Art Resurrected from the Catacombs

Wayne Pascall

Contents

Chapter One

Understanding the Catacombs

Understanding the Catacombs

The catacombs are an extensive network of underground burial places that were used primarily during the early Christian era. These subterranean passageways, often found on the outskirts of ancient cities, served as a final resting place for the deceased. The term "catacomb" itself originates from the Latin "catacumbas," which refers to a particular set of Roman burial chambers near the Appian Way. Over time, however, it has come to denote any similar underground cemetery. These labyrinthine complexes were not merely holes in the ground; they were carefully constructed and organized with narrow corridors leading to family tombs, larger rooms for communal burials, and sometimes even chapels for worship and commemoration. The walls of these passageways were lined with loculi (small burial niches), cubicula (mortuary chapels), and arcosolia (arched recesses for sarcophagi).

The catacombs are particularly associated with Rome, where over sixty have been discovered, but they can also be found in other parts of Italy and across the Mediterranean region including in Naples, Alexandria in Egypt, and Carthage in Tunisia. Their construction was a response to both practical and religious needs: land was expensive and scarce within city limits, so burials within city walls were limited. Moreover, early Christians preferred burial over cremation as it aligned with their belief in bodily resurrection.

The Origins and Purpose of the Catacombs

The origins of the catacombs date back to the 2nd century AD when Christianity was still a minority religion under Roman rule. Initially, Christians met and buried their dead in secret due to sporadic persecutions by Roman authorities who viewed Christianity as a threat to traditional Roman religious practices. As Christianity grew more accepted towards the end of the 2nd century, wealthier Christian families began constructing private burial sites beneath their land outside city walls. These sites would eventually expand into community cemeteries as members sought collective solace in death as they had in life. The purpose of these catacombs extended beyond mere interment; they became sacred spaces where believers could safely practice their faith away from public scrutiny. They held funeral banquets called 'agape' feasts to honor martyrs and saints on their death anniversaries—these gatherings reinforced community bonds among Christians.

Furthermore, during periods when Christianity was outlawed or frowned upon by Roman authorities, these underground sanctuaries offered refuge where Christians could conduct services undetected. This clandestine use underscores how integral catacombs were not only for burial but also for maintaining Christian worship traditions during times of oppression.

The Significance of the Catacombs in Early Christianity

In early Christianity's formative years, when its followers faced intermittent persecution from Roman authorities who demanded allegiance to pagan gods and emperor worship, catacombs played a crucial role in preserving Christian identity and practices. These subterranean networks provided more than just physical shelter; they symbolized hope amidst adversity—a place where faith could continue unimpeded by external threats. The very act of burying their dead according to Christian rites was an assertion of belief against prevailing pagan customs that favored cremation. Moreover, within these hidden depths emerged some of early Christianity's most poignant art forms—frescoes depicting biblical scenes such as Daniel in the lion's den or Jonah being swallowed by a whale served both didactic purposes teaching stories from scriptures—and expressed defiant hope through symbolic representation like anchors or doves signifying salvation or peace respectively.

This artwork wasn't merely decorative; it functioned as part of apologetics—the defense and proof of Christian doctrine against critics—by visually conveying theological concepts such as resurrection or eternal life which might otherwise be difficult for illiterate believers to grasp through text alone. Additionally, inscriptions accompanying these images often included prayers or expressions affirming faith which further solidified group identity among early Christians who visited these sacred spaces either for funerary purposes or clandestine worship gatherings during times when open practice posed significant risk.

Understanding catacombs provides insight into how early Christians navigated complex social landscapes marked by fluctuating degrees of tolerance towards their emerging religion while simultaneously carving out spaces—both literal and metaphorical—for sustaining nurturing nascent communities bound together shared beliefs rituals despite external pressures conform dominant cultural norms day.

Chapter Two

Exploring the Catacombs

A **Glimpse into the Past**

The catacombs, a labyrinth of underground burial places, offer a unique window into early Christian life and death. These subterranean passageways, primarily found surrounding the ancient city of Rome, served as both tombs and clandestine worship spaces for Christians from the ***2nd to the 5th century AD***. The origins of these catacombs are rooted in practicality and necessity; land was scarce and expensive, so early Christians sought an alternative for their dead. Moreover, their use reflected a distinct departure from Roman cremation practices in favor of burial, aligning with Christian belief in bodily resurrection.

The significance of the catacombs extends beyond their practical use. They became sacred spaces where believers could safely gather during times of persecution. The very walls that enclosed the remains of martyrs and saints were also adorned with symbols and artwork that expressed a rich theological tapestry and hope in eternal life. Exploring these catacombs today is akin to walking through a gallery of early Christian faith.

Early Christian Art Discovered in the Catacombs

Within these shadowy corridors lies some of the earliest known Christian art. Frescoes, sculptures, and inscriptions discovered here provide invaluable insights into early Christian iconography and liturgy. This art is characterized by its simplicity and symbolic nature; it often incorporates biblical themes such as salvation history or depicts scenes from both Old and New Testament narratives. One can find representations ranging from ***the Good Shepherd*** carrying a lost sheep—symbolizing Christ's care for his followers—to depictions of biblical stories like Jonah being swallowed by a great fish, which paralleled Christ's death and resurrection.

*"The Good Shepherd" art found in the Catacomb of
Priscilla, Rome.*

Early Christian art styles evolved over time but maintained an emphasis on conveying religious messages rather than aesthetic perfection. Byzantine influences began to permeate this art form as Christianity became more established within the empire. Mosaics with intricate patterns and vivid colors started to appear alongside earlier frescoes, reflecting both an evolution in artistic technique and theological sophistication.

Symbols like the ***ichthys (fish)***, ***anchor***, or ***alpha and omega*** were frequently used as cryptic signs that identified believers while evading detection by Roman authorities. These symbols not only communicated faith but also provided comfort to those who risked their lives for their beliefs. Christian art within these catacombs served another critical function—it acted as part of apologetics or defenses of Christianity against pagan critiques. Through visual narratives, artists could express complex theological concepts accessible to those who may not have been literate or well-versed in scripture.

Unveiling Hidden Chambers

As archaeologists continue to explore these ancient sites, new chambers are uncovered that reveal even more about early Christian practices. The discovery process is painstakingly delicate due to the fragile nature of these environments; however, each new chamber can potentially hold untold treasures that have lain undisturbed for centuries. Restoration efforts play a crucial role in preserving this heritage for future generations while allowing us to appreciate its original beauty. Techniques vary depending on material conditions—from consolidating crumbling frescoes using modern adhesives to employing digital technology that reconstructs damaged artworks virtually. Despite challenges such as humidity control or limited access due to structural instability, restorations have successfully revived many masterpieces once thought lost forever. These triumphs not only restore physical artifacts but also breathe life back into stories they tell about our collective past.

Insights from Archaeological Studies

Archaeological studies within catacombs have yielded profound insights into early Christianity's development under Roman rule—a period marked by sporadic yet brutal persecutions. Art found here often contains hidden messages serving as forms of resistance against oppressive authorities while reinforcing group identity among believers. For instance, coded language within inscriptions or subtle alterations in traditional iconography allowed Christians to communicate openly without fear of reprisal from Roman officials who might otherwise misunderstand these signals' true meanings. Moreover, archaeological evidence has illuminated aspects such as burial customs—revealing how social status influenced tomb size or placement— and dietary habits gleaned from remnants found at agape feasts held within these sacred spaces.

These studies contribute significantly towards understanding how Christianity transitioned from a persecuted minority religion into one eventually embraced by an empire—shaping Western civilization profoundly along its journey through time.

Chapter Three

The Early Christian Church

Spread of Christianity in the Roman Empire

During the time of the Roman Empire, Christianity experienced a remarkable spread throughout the region. This rapid expansion can be attributed to several historical factors and contexts that contributed to the growth and popularity of the faith. One of the key elements that contributed to the spread of Christianity in the Roman Empire was the existence of an extensive network of roads and trade routes. The Romans had constructed a vast network of roads that facilitated travel and trade across their empire. These roads not only promoted efficient communication and transportation but also provided opportunities for the spread of ideas, including Christianity.

Another significant factor that contributed to the spread of Christianity in the Roman Empire was the presence of a common language.

The widespread use of Greek as the lingua franca of the Eastern Roman Empire enabled Christian apostles and missionaries to communicate their message effectively to a diverse audience. The availability of translations of religious texts into Greek further facilitated the dissemination of Christian beliefs. The political environment of the Roman Empire also played a crucial role in the spread of Christianity. The Romans practiced religious syncretism, which allowed the incorporation of new gods and belief systems into their existing pantheon. This tolerance towards different religious practices meant that Christianity could coexist alongside other religions in the empire.

Christianity offered the appeal of a personal relationship with God, which resonated with individuals seeking a more personal and meaningful religious experience. The promise of salvation and eternal life after death also attracted many people to the faith. Furthermore, the early Christians' commitment to acts of charity and community support made a significant impact on the population. This commitment to caring for the poor and marginalized served as a powerful testament to the transformative power of the Christian faith. Although the spread of Christianity in the Roman Empire faced many challenges, such as persecution and opposition from both religious and political authorities, the faith continued to flourish. The early Christian community demonstrated remarkable resilience and perseverance in promoting their beliefs, ultimately paving the way for Christianity to become the dominant religion in the Roman Empire.

Persecution of Christians

Persecution of Christians during the early centuries was a grim reality that profoundly affected their beliefs and practices. This section will delve into the depths of the challenges faced by Christians and the lasting impact it had on their faith. The early Christians faced persecution from various sources, including the Roman Empire and local authorities. They were often targeted for their refusal to worship Roman gods and participate in pagan rituals. This subchapter will explore the reasons behind the persecution and the methods used to suppress the growing Christian community.

During this tumultuous period, Christians had to find ways to practice their faith in secret. They sought refuge in the catacombs as a safe haven for worship and burial. These catacombs, underground burial sites, became not only a place to remember and honor the dead but also a place where Christians could gather in secrecy to worship and strengthen their beliefs. The catacombs played a crucial role in preserving Christian art and symbols. In this subchapter, we will examine the various artistic expressions found in these underground tunnels. From intricate frescoes depicting scenes from the Bible to symbols of faith such as the fish and the anchor, the catacombs are a treasure trove of Christian history and art.

Exploring the catacombs also provides insights into the daily life of early Christians. Their burials, epitaphs, and funerary customs reveal their unwavering devotion to their faith and their hope in the resurrection. By studying these aspects, we gain a deeper understanding of the challenges they faced and the strength of their convictions. Join us as we journey through the history of persecution, discovering the resilience of the early Christians and the significant role the catacombs played in upholding their beliefs and practices.

Role of the Catacombs in Early Christianity

The catacombs hold great significance as a place for communal worship, burial rituals, and the preservation of Christian identity. In early Christianity, the catacombs served as an important gathering place for believers to come together and worship in secret. The catacombs were also used as burial grounds, where Christians would inter their loved ones. This practice of burying fellow believers in the catacombs not only fulfilled the religious duty of honoring the dead, but also reinforced their shared identity as followers of Christ. Additionally, the catacombs played a crucial role in preserving the Christian faith during a time of persecution. As Christians faced opposition from the Roman Empire, the catacombs provided a safe haven to practice their faith and maintain their Christian identity. The underground tunnels and chambers allowed believers to gather in secret, away from the prying eyes of the authorities.

Alongside their practical purposes, the catacombs also served as a canvas for catacomb art, which played a vital role in fostering Christian beliefs and communicating the message of salvation. Catacombs art can be found in the form of frescoes, sculptures, mosaics, and inscriptions. These artistic expressions depicted various scenes from the Bible, such as the miracles of Jesus, the Last Supper, and the stories of martyrs. The artwork not only served as a visual representation of

Christian teachings, but also provided inspiration and encouragement for believers.

The catacomb art also helped to reinforce the Christian identity in times of persecution. By depicting scenes of martyrdom and the promise of eternal life, the artwork served as a reminder of the ultimate sacrifice made by early Christians and the hope that awaited them in the afterlife.

Chapter Four

Early Christian Art in the Catacombs

Early Christian Art in the Catacombs Discoveries and Interpretations

The catacombs of ancient Rome, a labyrinthine network of underground burial places, have long fascinated historians and art enthusiasts alike. Their discovery provided an unprecedented window into the lives and beliefs of early Christians. Initially serving as burial sites due to space constraints and the prohibitive cost of land, these subterranean chambers became a canvas for some of the earliest Christian art. The interpretation of catacomb art has evolved over time. Initially, scholars viewed these images purely as religious symbols or as mere decoration for tombs. However, further study revealed that they were also a form of communication among believers who were often persecuted for their faith. The artwork served not only to convey

Christian doctrine but also to offer hope and solidarity in times of distress.

One notable example is the ***image of Jonah being swallowed by a great fish***, which was interpreted as a symbol of resurrection and salvation reflecting the story's outcome where Jonah emerges safely after three days—a parallel to Christ's resurrection. Similarly, depictions of the Good Shepherd represented Jesus' care for his followers. As archaeologists continue to uncover new sections of catacombs and employ advanced technologies such as laser scanning and 3D modeling, our understanding deepens. These methods allow us to preserve delicate frescoes digitally before they deteriorate further due to exposure to light and air.

Unveiling the Beauty: Early Christian Art Styles

The beauty inherent in early Christian art found within the catacombs is characterized by its simplicity and symbolic nature. Unlike their pagan contemporaries who celebrated human form with realistic portrayals in sculpture and painting, early Christians focused on conveying spiritual truths through more abstract means. This period saw a blend of styles influenced by Roman artistic traditions with emerging Christian themes. Frescoes depicted biblical scenes using bright colors but often lacked perspective or depth—techniques that would later be refined during the Renaissance.

One distinctive feature was the use of iconic symbols such as ***the chi-rho monogram (□)***, which combined the first two letters of Christ's name in Greek, signifying his presence. **The peacock** was another common motif symbolizing immortality due to an ancient belief that its flesh did not decay. Artists during this time were less concerned with anatomical accuracy than with creating an immediate visual impact that conveyed a message quickly and effectively to those who might not be literate but could understand pictorial representations.

Byzantine Art: A Testament to Faith and Devotion

Byzantine art emerged from early Christian art forms around the 4th century AD when Constantine moved his capital from Rome to Byzantium (later Constantinople). This new style reflected both continuity with earlier traditions and significant developments that would influence Western art for centuries. Byzantine artists perfected mosaic techniques, creating intricate designs using tiny pieces of colored glass or stone set into plaster—a medium well-suited for decorating churches' domes and apses. These glittering mosaics often depicted Christ Pantocrator (Ruler of All) or scenes from His life, emphasizing divine majesty rather than human vulnerability.

Another hallmark was iconography—religious images used in worship— which became central to Byzantine spirituality despite periods where their use was hotly contested (Iconoclasm). Icons were believed not just as representations but windows into heaven; thus they were created following strict conventions ensuring consistency across time and space. The architecture itself became part of this devotional artistry with structures like **Hagia Sophia** showcasing how space could be transformed into a reflection of heavenly glory through domes rising heavenward amidst cascading light—an architectural metaphor for God's kingdom on earth.

In conclusion, each era within early Christian art—from catacomb paintings through Byzantine mosaics—revealed layers about how these communities understood themselves in relation to their faith under varying circumstances including persecution, doctrinal development, cultural exchange, and technological innovation—all contributing towards an enduring legacy still appreciated today.

Chapter Five

Symbols of Faith in Christian Art

The Christian Fish and Other Iconography

Christian iconography is a visual language that has been used since the earliest days of the faith to communicate religious ideas, tell stories from the Bible, and express aspects of Christian belief. Among these symbols, the **Christian fish**, or *ichthys*, stands out as one of the most recognizable. The Greek word for fish, "ichthys," was used as an acronym for "***Iesous Christos Theou Yios Soter***," translating to "Jesus Christ, Son of God, Savior." This symbol was particularly useful during times of persecution when Christians needed a covert way to identify each other.

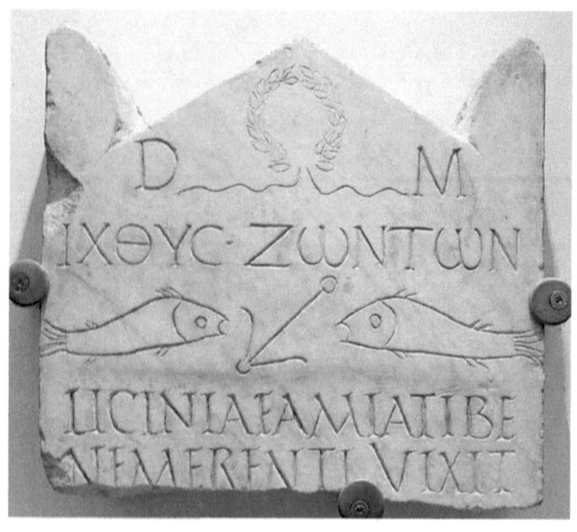

Beyond the fish, early Christians adopted a variety of other symbols. ***The anchor*** was another early Christian symbol that represented hope and steadfastness in faith; it also resembled a cross but was less conspicuous during periods of persecution. ***The peacock*** was used to symbolize immortality because of an ancient belief that its flesh did not decay after death. Similarly, ***the phoenix*** served as a metaphor for resurrection and eternal life.

The use of iconography extended into liturgical objects and architecture. Chalices, patens, and even fonts were often adorned with symbols such as vines (representing Christ as the true vine) or wheat (symbolizing the bread of life). Churches themselves were designed with an eastward orientation towards the rising sun—a symbol for Christ's resurrection—and often incorporated intricate mosaics depicting biblical scenes or saints. In addition to these more common symbols, there were also more esoteric ones like the ***Ouroboros***—an ancient image of a snake eating its own tail— that signified eternity and the soul's immortality. Early Christians borrowed this symbol from pagan traditions and imbued it with their own meanings.

These symbols served not only as identifiers but also as tools for meditation and reflection on spiritual truths. They provided comfort in times of distress and served as focal points during prayer and worship.

Symbolism in Early Christian Art

Early Christian art is rich with symbolism that conveyed complex theological concepts in a time when literacy was not widespread among all social classes. This art often had to serve multiple purposes: instructing believers in their faith, providing an aid for worship, commemorating martyrs and saints, and sometimes offering coded messages during times when Christianity was outlawed. One prominent example is found in depictions of Christ as the Good Shepherd—a motif borrowed from earlier Greco-Roman culture—which resonated deeply with early Christians who saw Jesus as their protector who would leave his flock to find one lost sheep. This image also communicated values such as care, leadership, sacrifice, and community.

Another significant aspect is how early Christian artists adapted existing Roman artistic styles while infusing them with new meaning. For instance, sarcophagi were decorated with scenes from scripture rather than traditional Roman motifs. These carvings could range from Jonah being swallowed by a whale—symbolizing death and resurrection—to Daniel in the lion's den— representing divine protection against oppression.

The ***use of light*** itself became symbolic within early Christian art; churches were constructed to allow natural light to play across mosaics or paintings at certain times of day or year—creating dynamic experiences that underscored theological themes about enlightenment or divine presence. Moreover, *colors* held symbolic value: gold represented heavenly glory; white indicated purity; purple stood for royalty (and thus Christ's kingship); red signified martyrdom or divine love; blue evoked heaven or truth; green symbolized life or rebirth.

Decoding Religious Imagery

Understanding religious imagery *requires knowledge* not only about what specific symbols represent but also about how they interact within a piece of art to convey deeper meanings. Decoding this imagery allows us to appreciate fully how art functioned within early Christianity—not just aesthetically but spiritually and educationally too. For instance, consider an image where Peter is depicted holding keys while Paul holds a book—the keys represent Peter's role in granting access to heaven (as per Jesus' words that he would give him "the keys of the kingdom"), while Paul's book signifies his contributions through epistles which form much of New Testament theology.

Similarly intricate are apse mosaics found in many churches where Christ might be surrounded by apostles or saints against a *golden background*— each figure carefully chosen for their particular significance to that community along with *inscriptions* that may quote relevant scripture passages adding layers upon layers of meaning intended for contemplation during worship services. Furthermore, deciphering religious imagery can reveal insights into historical contexts—for example, understanding how images evolved over time, can reflect shifts in theological emphases or responses to heretical movements within Christianity. Artists often employed *typology*—a method where Old Testament events are seen as prefigurations (or types) for New Testament events—to draw connections between disparate parts of scripture creating rich tapestries woven together by shared motifs reinforcing doctrinal teachings about salvation history. An understanding of these influences helps us understand art and icons found in the catacombs.

Decoding religious imagery isn't just about identifying individual elements but engaging with them holistically—as partaking in dialogue across time between artist believer theologian, historian and the masses.

Chapter Six

Resurrection and Redemption in Art

Depictions of Christ's Resurrection

In the rich history of Christian art, one of the most significant events depicted is the resurrection of Jesus Christ. This pivotal moment in Christian theology holds immense importance and has been portrayed in various artistic representations found in catacombs around the world. Let's explore the depictions of Christ's resurrection and delve into their theological significance.

Portrayals of Martyrdom

The catacombs of Rome are fascinating burial sites that date back to the early centuries of Christianity. These underground tunnels served as a resting place for the deceased, but they also hold important clues about the early Christian community's beliefs, struggles, and identity. One of the recurring motifs found in the catacombs is the portrayal of Christian martyrs and their ultimate sacrifice for their faith. When examining the depictions of martyrdom in catacomb art, we can gain insights into the significance of martyrdom in shaping early Christian beliefs and identity. The artists of these artworks sought to honor the memory of these courageous individuals who willingly faced persecution and death for their commitment to Christ.

The catacomb art portrays various scenes of martyrdom, vividly capturing the courage and faith of these early Christians. In these depictions, we see scenes of believers being thrown to the lions in the Roman amphitheaters, others being crucified, and some even being burned at the stake. These graphic representations serve as a reminder of the sacrifices made by these individuals and the challenges they faced as followers of Christ. By examining the portrayal of Christian martyrs in catacomb art, we can gain a deeper understanding of the early Christian community's unwavering faith and dedication to their beliefs. These depictions not only serve as a visual tribute to the martyrs but also inspire and encourage believers in their own faith journeys.

The role of martyrdom in shaping early Christian identity and beliefs cannot be overstated. The acts of martyrdom represented in catacomb art were not merely instances of persecution, but they were seen as a powerful witness to the world. The early Christians believed that the blood of the martyrs was seed, meaning that their sacrifices would ultimately lead to the growth and spread of the Christian faith. These depictions of martyrdom conveyed a message of strength and perseverance in the face of adversity. They served as a reminder to the early Christians that their faith was worth sacrificing for, and that their commitment to Christ could not be shaken. The martyrs became symbols of hope and inspiration, encouraging others to remain steadfast in their faith. Furthermore, the portrayal of martyrdom in catacomb art also played a crucial role in apologetics, or the defense of the Christian faith. In a time when Christians faced persecution and were often misunderstood by the larger Greco-Roman society, these depictions served as a powerful tool in explaining and defending Christian beliefs and practices.

Overall, the portrayal of Christian martyrs and their sacrifices in catacomb art provides us with a glimpse into the early Christian community's deep commitment to their faith. These depictions not only honor the memory of these courageous individuals but also inspire and encourage believers today. The catacomb art serves as a testament to the power of faith and the enduring impact of martyrdom on shaping early Christian identity and beliefs.

Themes of Forgiveness and Redemption

Forgiveness and redemption are central themes in the Christian faith, and they have been depicted in various forms of art throughout history. Catacomb art, in particular, provides a unique insight into the representation of these themes. Let's explore how forgiveness and redemption are depicted in catacomb art and their significance in conveying the central message of the Christian faith. One of the prominent themes that appear in catacomb art is forgiveness. This theme is often portrayed through scenes depicting biblical stories, such as the parable of the prodigal son or Jesus' forgiveness of the adulterous woman. These depictions emphasize the compassion and mercy of God, highlighting the belief that forgiveness is attainable for all who seek it.

Catacomb art also portrays the concept of redemption. This theme is exemplified through images of Jesus' crucifixion and resurrection. The crucifixion represents the ultimate act of redemption, as Jesus sacrificed himself to save humanity from sin. The resurrection, on the other hand, symbolizes the victory over death and the promise of eternal salvation. Catacomb art often includes symbols that represent forgiveness and redemption. For example, the image of a dove is used to signify the Holy Spirit, who is believed to guide and empower individuals to seek forgiveness and embrace redemption. Similarly, the image of a fish, which has been historically associated with Christ, symbolizes the transformative power of forgiveness and redemption.

The representation of forgiveness and redemption in catacomb art holds immense significance in conveying the central message of Christian faith. These themes serve as reminders of God's love, mercy, and the possibility of spiritual renewal. They encourage believers to seek forgiveness for their sins and find redemption through Christ's sacrifice. Moreover, the inclusion of forgiveness and redemption in catacomb art serves as a source of hope and comfort for believers facing trials and hardships. It reminds them that, no matter the depth of their transgressions, forgiveness is available, and redemption is within reach. Through the visual representations of forgiveness and redemption in catacomb art, individuals are invited to reflect on their own lives and consider the transformative power of these themes. They inspire believers to live with compassion, forgiveness, and gratitude, and to extend the same grace to others.

Chapter Seven

Christian Art as Apologetics

Visual Defense in Early Christianity

In the nascent stages of Christianity, art served as a powerful tool for expressing and defending the faith amidst a predominantly pagan society. The early Christians were often marginalized and persecuted, leading them to seek refuge and solace in their beliefs. This is where the catacombs come into play—a subterranean network of burial places beneath Rome that provided not only a final resting place for the dead but also a canvas for Christian expression. The catacombs were adorned with frescoes, sculptures, and symbols that conveyed Christian narratives and theology. These visual elements served as an unspoken defense of their faith. For instance, images of Christ as the Good Shepherd or depictions of biblical stories like Jonah and the Whale offered hope and reassurance to believers who faced oppression above ground.

Moreover, these artworks were not merely decorative; they were catechetical tools used to educate and reinforce the doctrines among Christians who may have been illiterate or new to the faith. The use of iconography such as the fish (Ichthys), which was an acronym for "Jesus Christ, Son of God, Savior," allowed believers to communicate their faith covertly in a society where open worship could lead to persecution. Art within these sacred spaces also reflected an apologetic stance against Roman religious practices. By emphasizing themes such as resurrection and eternal life—concepts absent from Roman funerary art—Christians visually asserted their distinct beliefs about death and the afterlife. Furthermore, early Christian art often incorporated elements from Greco-Roman culture but repurposed them with Christian significance. This strategic approach not only made Christianity more accessible to converts familiar with pagan symbols but also demonstrated how Christian doctrine could transcend cultural boundaries.

Role of Art in Promoting Christian Beliefs

As Christianity grew from its roots in Judaism into a religion that spanned across cultures, art became an essential medium for promoting its beliefs. During this period, art was one of the most effective ways to communicate stories and theological concepts due to widespread illiteracy. Christianity's message was revolutionary in its emphasis on love, sacrifice, humility, and redemption—themes powerfully conveyed through visual arts. Scenes from Christ's life—the Nativity, Crucifixion, Resurrection—and images of saints martyred for their unwavering devotion brought biblical narratives to life for believers. The role of art extended beyond mere representation; it functioned as a formative influence on Christian identity. Churches adorned with mosaics depicting scenes from Scripture invited reflection and meditation on divine mysteries. Stained glass windows illuminated sacred spaces with colorful light while narrating salvation history.

Byzantine art deserves special mention here due to its profound impact on promoting Christian beliefs. Its distinctive style—with gold backgrounds symbolizing divine glory and frontal figures inviting direct engagement— served both aesthetic purposes and doctrinal instruction. Icons became "windows into heaven," offering believers tangible access points for veneration and prayer. Art also played a crucial role during times when heresies threatened church unity. Orthodox imagery reinforced correct teachings about Christ's nature—fully human and fully divine—as defined by ecumenical councils like Nicaea (325 AD) and Chalcedon (451 AD).

Impact on Contemporary Christian Apologetics

In contemporary times, apologetics has evolved beyond verbal argumentation into realms that include multimedia experiences encompassing film, music, literature—and still prominently—visual arts. Modern apologists recognize that we live in an image-saturated culture where visual literacy is paramount; thus they harness this medium's potential for engaging hearts and minds toward faith. Contemporary artists create works inspired by traditional themes yet rendered in styles that resonate with today's audiences. They might reinterpret classical motifs or craft entirely new visuals that speak directly to current societal issues while rooted in timeless truths. Christian filmmakers produce movies that tackle complex theological questions through narrative storytelling—a form of visual apologetics reaching millions worldwide. Similarly, graphic novels retelling biblical stories or exploring spiritual themes have emerged as powerful tools for evangelization among younger generations more attuned to visual learning.

Moreover, digital media has opened up unprecedented opportunities for disseminating Christian artwork globally at rapid speeds—an electronic echo of ancient catacomb paintings' silent witness across centuries. In addition to creating new works, there is also a movement dedicated to preserving historical pieces through restoration efforts—a testament not only to our heritage but also an ongoing dialogue between past wisdom informing present understandings. Through exhibitions showcasing restored masterpieces or virtual tours allowing remote access into ancient churches adorned with frescoes once hidden from public view due to persecution or neglect—we see how historical apologetics continues shaping contemporary discourse around faith matters.

In conclusion, whether through ancient frescoes hidden underground or modern films projected onto screens worldwide—art remains an enduring vessel carrying forward Christianity's message across time: A visual defense transformed into a universal language speaking volumes without uttering a single word.

Theology and Belief Reflected in Art

When exploring the rich history of Christian art, one cannot overlook the fascinating imagery and symbolism found in the catacombs. These underground burial sites were not only places of remembrance but also served as crucial spaces for early Christians to express and reinforce their faith. In this section, we will analyze the theological concepts and beliefs reflected in the art of the catacombs. Through the intricate artwork found in the catacombs, we can gain insight into the theo-logical concepts and beliefs of early Christians. One common theme is the portrayal of biblical narratives, particularly those centered around salvation and the life of Jesus Christ. These visual representations served as important reminders of the core teachings of Christianity.

For example, the image of Christ as the Good Shepherd was a beloved symbol for early Christians. This portrayal demonstrated not only Jesus' care and protection for his believers but also emphasized the message of redemption and salvation. Such imagery reassured the faithful during times of persecution and uncertainty. In addition to biblical narratives, catacomb art also often incorporated symbols that represented key theological concepts. The use of the fish symbol, known as the Ichthys, held great significance for early Christians. It not only symbolized their faith but also conveyed the idea of Christ as the divine Savior. This symbol carried a powerful message of hope and unity for believers in the face of adversity.

Religious iconography played a crucial role in expressing and rein-forcing the Christian faith within the catacombs. The use of symbolic imagery allowed early Christians to communicate complex theological concepts in a visual and accessible manner. Furthermore, the presence of these religious symbols served as a shared language among believers. In a time when Christianity faced persecution and was viewed with suspicion by the Roman Empire, these visual representations helped foster a sense of community and unity among Christians. Religious iconography in the catacombs also served as a source of inspiration and encouragement. The depictions of martyrs and saints reminded believers of the ultimate sacrifice made for their faith and encouraged them to persevere in the face of adversity.

Impact of Catacomb Art on Christian Worship

Throughout history, art has held great significance in various aspects of human culture. In the context of Christianity, artistic representations have played a vital role in invoking a sense of devotion and reverence among believers. One particular form of art that has had a profound impact on Christian worship practices is catacomb art. The catacombs, underground burial chambers used by early Christians, served as spaces for both interment and worship. These underground chambers provided a sanctuary for believers to gather and practice their faith in times of persecution. Within the catacombs, various art forms emerged, reflecting the beliefs and values of the early Christian community.

The influence of catacomb art on Christian worship practices can be seen in the way it conveyed important theological concepts, fostered a sense of community, and provided a visual representation of the faith. Many of these artworks depicted scenes from the Bible, such as the miracles of Jesus, the Last Supper, or stories of martyrdom. The impact of catacomb art on Christian worship can be observed through the symbolisms and motifs used in these artworks. For example, the image of the Good Shepherd represented Jesus Christ as the guide and protector of his flock, instilling a sense of comfort and assurance in the hearts of believers. The use of the fish symbol, known as the Ichthys, served as a secret sign of recognition among early Christians and conveyed the message of their faith. Moreover, catacomb art served as a means of educating and reinforcing Christian beliefs to the illiterate members of the community. Through visual representations, important narratives from the Bible were communicated, allowing individuals to engage with the stories and teachings profoundly.

Artistic representations in the catacombs also played a crucial role in creating a sacred atmosphere conducive to worship. The use of symbols, colors, and imagery evoked a sense of awe and reverence among believers, enhancing their spiritual experience. The very act of descending into the underground catacombs, away from the distractions of the external world, facilitated a deeper connection with God. Catacomb art has significantly influenced the development of Christian worship practices. Its theological significance, its ability to foster community, and its role in invoking devotion and reverence all contribute to its enduring impact. The artworks found in the catacombs provide a glimpse into the early Christian community's beliefs, values, and devotion to their faith, which continues to inspire and resonate with believers today.

Comparisons with Other Christian Art

Comparisons can provide valuable insights into the distinctiveness and significance of catacomb art within the broader artistic tradition. Mosaics and frescoes have long been revered as prominent forms of Christian art, known for their intricate designs and vibrant colors. Mosaics, composed of small pieces of colored glass or stone, were often used to decorate the floors, walls, and ceilings of churches and basilicas. They depicted biblical scenes, saints, and symbols, and were highly regarded for their artistic beauty and religious symbolism.

Frescoes, on the other hand, involved painting directly on wet plaster, allowing the pigments to seep into the wall and become a part of the surface. Churches and religious buildings would often commission frescoes to adorn their interiors, portraying religious narratives or illustrating theological concepts. Frescoes were renowned for their vivid colors and detailed brushwork, creating a sense of life-like realism. While catacomb art shares similarities with mosaics and frescoes in its religious subject matter and symbolism, there are some notable differences that set it apart. Catacombs were underground burial sites for early Christians, and the art found within these burial chambers served a different purpose than the more public and decorative nature of mosaics and frescoes.

Catacomb art often consisted of simple and humble depictions of Christian symbols and stories, carved or painted onto the walls and ceilings of the burial chambers. These images were created by ordinary Christians, conveying their faith and providing solace in times of persecution and hardship. Unlike the grandeur and opulence of mosaics and frescoes, catacomb art reflected the everyday lives and struggles of early Christians. Despite its simplicity, catacomb art played a significant role in the development of Christian iconography and the preservation of Christian history. These underground artworks served as a testimony to the faith and resilience of early Christians, and they also provided a visual means of passing down biblical narratives and teachings.

Catacomb art often displayed a distinct Eastern influence, with its use of symbols such as the Chi-Rho, the Good Shepherd, and the fish. These symbols, drawn from the traditions of the Eastern Mediterranean, reflected the cultural and geographical contexts in which early Christianity thrived. Comparing catacomb art with mosaics and frescoes reveals both similarities and distinctive features. While mosaics and frescoes were celebrated for their artistic beauty and grandeur, catacomb art possessed a simplicity and humility that conveyed the everyday faith and struggles of early Christians. These underground artworks served as important visual tools for the preservation of Christian history and the transmission of biblical narratives.

Chapter Eight

Restoration of Catacomb Art

Preserving the Past: The Importance of Restoration

The catacombs, an intricate network of underground burial places, are a testament to the resilience and ingenuity of early Christians. These subterranean galleries not only served as final resting places but also as sanctuaries for worship and safe havens during periods of persecution. The art found within these catacombs is invaluable, providing insight into the beliefs, traditions, and daily life of early Christian communities. Restoration plays a crucial role in preserving this heritage. Without it, we risk losing the connection to a pivotal era in human history. Catacomb art is particularly vulnerable due to its age and the fragile nature of its materials. Over time, frescoes fade, moisture damages structures, and external factors such as pollution or vandalism can further threaten these ancient artworks.

The importance of restoration extends beyond mere aesthetics; it is about safeguarding cultural identity. For many believers, these images are not just decorations but representations of faith that have endured through centuries. Restoring them allows current and future generations to witness the evolution of Christian iconography and understand its context within the broader tapestry of world religions. Restoration contributes to historical scholarship. It enables researchers to study techniques and materials used by early artists, which in turn provides insights into technological advancements and trade practices of the time. Each restored piece adds another chapter to our collective story, bridging gaps between past civilizations and modern society. Furthermore, restored catacomb art has economic implications through tourism. Visitors from around the globe flock to see these ancient marvels firsthand—a boon for local economies that often rely on cultural heritage sites for income. In essence, restoration serves as a conduit between past and present— allowing us to experience history tangibly while ensuring its survival for those who will write our future histories.

Methods Used in Restoring Catacomb Art

Restoring catacomb art is a meticulous process that combines traditional techniques with modern technology. The primary goal is always preservation—maintaining the integrity of original works while halting further deterioration.

- One common method involves ***cleaning surfaces gently*** using soft brushes or sponges with distilled water or mild solvents that do not react with paint or stone. This step removes accumulated dirt and biological growths without damaging underlying artwork.

- ***Consolidation*** is another critical technique where weakened areas are reinforced using adhesives or fillers compatible with original materials. This process stabilizes fragile sections preventing collapse or loss due to crumbling substrates. In some cases where frescoes have faded significantly or suffered damage beyond simple cleaning or consolidation efforts, in-filling may be necessary. Here conservators carefully recreate missing portions based on extensive research into styles, colors, and motifs consistent with the period's artistry.

- ***Digital technology*** also plays an increasingly significant role in restoration projects today. High-resolution imaging allows experts to analyze artworks without physical contact—identifying areas needing attention while minimizing handling risks associated with delicate pieces.

- ***Laser cleaning*** has emerged as a revolutionary tool capable of removing encrustations without abrasion—a particular advantage when dealing with soft volcanic rock commonly found in Roman catacombs.

- Lastly, ***environmental control systems*** are installed within catacombs themselves to regulate temperature and humidity levels—key factors in preventing future degradation caused by climate fluctuations.

Each method requires skilled professionals trained in conservation science—an interdisciplinary field encompassing chemistry biology archaeology fine arts—to ensure successful restorations that honor both historical accuracy and artistic value inherent within each piece preserved beneath Rome's streets.

Challenges and Triumphs: Restoring Fragile Masterpieces

The task of restoring catacomb art comes laden with challenges unique due largely to the environment in which they reside—underground spaces subject to fluctuating conditions pose constant threats to preservation efforts undertaken therein. One major challenge lies in the inherent fragility of the mediums used to create artworks themselves; frescoes and murals painted directly onto damp walls are prone to erosion over time making them especially susceptible to damage even the slightest misstep during conservation work, could result in irreversible harm. Another obstacle faced by restorers access; is that narrow corridors and low ceilings make maneuverability difficult requiring specialized equipment techniques to navigate tight confines safely and effectively carry out necessary procedures.

Despite these difficulties, triumphs abound in realm restoration; each successfully conserved piece represents victory against the ravages of time elements providing a tangible link to ancestors' spiritual lives. A notable success story Sistine Chapel Rome where team international experts spent years painstakingly cleaning Michelangelo's ceiling frescoes restoring them to their former glory process revealed vibrant colors and details previously obscured by centuries' worth of grime smoke candle soot testament skill dedication involved such endeavors.

Similarly, ongoing projects like Catacombs Priscilla continue to demonstrate potential rewards come perseverance innovation face adversity; here advanced imaging tools being employed uncover hidden layers of paint and reveal stories long thought lost sands of time. These successes not only celebrate technical achievements but also emotional resonance felt upon witnessing rebirth artifacts once thought beyond salvation they stand as beacons of hope to all who believe the power of the human spirit overcomes the greatest odds to preserve beauty knowledge posterity.

Chapter Nine

Persecution and Resistance through Art

Roman Persecution of Christians: A Dark Period in History

The Roman persecution of Christians stands as one of the most somber chapters in human history. It was a period marked by fear, brutality, and bloodshed, where professing faith in Christ could lead to a death sentence. The early Christian community faced intermittent periods of intense persecution from Roman authorities who viewed the new sect with suspicion and hostility. This animosity was rooted in the Christians' refusal to worship the Roman gods and the Emperor, which was considered an act of treason against the state.

The Great Fire of Rome in 64 AD under Emperor Nero marked one of the first major persecutions, where Christians were scapegoated for the disaster. Tacitus, a Roman historian, documented that Nero inflicted grotesque tortures on Christians, including being torn by dogs or crucified. Some were even used as human torches at night. Subsequent emperors like Domitian, Decius, Valerian, and Diocletian continued these persecutions with varying degrees of intensity and geographical scope. During these dark times, Christianity continued to spread despite—or perhaps because of—the blood of martyrs. The Church Fathers wrote apologies defending Christianity while others like Tertullian proclaimed that "the blood of martyrs is the seed of the Church." These persecutions also led to significant theological developments as believers sought to understand suffering and divine providence.

Hidden Messages: Christian Art as a Form of Resistance

In response to this oppressive environment, early Christians developed subtle methods to express and sustain their faith—one such method was through art. Christian art during this period often contained hidden messages that conveyed spiritual truths while eluding detection by Roman authorities. One example is the use of common symbols with dual meanings. **The fish (Ichthys)**, for instance, became an emblem for Christ because its Greek letters form an acrostic for *"Jesus Christ, Son of God, Savior."* To non-Christians it appeared innocuous; however, for believers, it signified their faith covertly. Similarly, images like anchors or doves carried connotations of hope and the Holy Spirit respectively but would not have been overtly associated with Christianity by outsiders.

Artists also employed biblical narratives that paralleled Christian experiences under persecution without directly referencing contemporary events. Scenes such as Daniel in the lion's den or Moses striking water from a rock resonated deeply with believers enduring trials yet remained ambiguous enough not to provoke further oppression. Moreover, early Christian art served as a means to educate and catechize members within their community who were often illiterate. Frescoes depicting scenes from Jesus' life or saints' martyrdoms provided visual theology lessons that reinforced doctrine and encouraged perseverance amidst suffering.

The Role of Catacomb Art in Preserving Christian Identity

Catacombs—underground burial places—played a pivotal role in preserving Christian identity during times when open worship could lead to execution. These subterranean labyrinths beneath Rome (and other cities) became sanctuaries for both the living and dead; they housed tombs but also served as clandestine meeting places for worship and instruction. The walls within the catacombs are adorned with frescoes that reflect early Christian beliefs and values. These artworks are more than mere decorations; they are profound expressions of faith crafted under perilous circumstances. They depict biblical stories emphasizing themes like resurrection (Jonah being vomited out by a whale), salvation (Noah's Ark), and eternal life (the Good Shepherd), among others—all reinforcing key tenets central to maintaining a distinct Christian identity amidst pagan culture.

Catacomb art also functioned as theological affirmations against heretical teachings that threatened unity within early Christianity itself—such as Gnosticism or Marcionism—which distorted traditional doctrines about Jesus' nature or Old Testament relevance. Furthermore, these sacred spaces allowed continuity between generations; they connected newer converts with those who had passed on before them through inscriptions commemorating deceased believers alongside depictions illustrating shared beliefs—a tangible link across time reinforcing communal bonds forged through shared adversity.

The Roman persecution catalyzed creative forms of resistance among Christians. Art became an essential vehicle for expressing forbidden faith subtly. The catacombs provided both physical refuge and spiritual sustenance through their rich iconography. Each element—persecution narrative, artistic expression under duress, catacomb sanctuary—interweaves into a tapestry illustrating how early Christians navigated existential threats while forging an enduring legacy through resilience articulated via artistry imbued with hope amidst despairing times.

Chapter Ten

Catacombs as Testaments of Faith

Theology and Belief Reflected in Art

When exploring the rich history of Christian art, one cannot overlook the fascinating imagery and symbolism found in the catacombs. These underground burial sites were not only places of remembrance but also served as crucial spaces for early Christians to express and reinforce their faith. In this section, we will analyze the theological concepts and beliefs reflected in the art of the catacombs. Through the intricate artwork found in the catacombs, we can gain insight into the theological concepts and beliefs of early Christians. One common theme is the portrayal of biblical narratives, particularly those centered around salvation and the life of Jesus Christ.

These visual representations served as important reminders of the core teachings of Christianity.

For example, the image of Christ as the Good Shepherd was a beloved symbol for early Christians. This portrayal demonstrated not only Jesus' care and protection for his believers but also emphasized the message of redemption and salvation. Such imagery reassured the faithful during times of persecution and uncertainty. In addition to biblical narratives, catacomb art also often incorporated symbols that represented key theological concepts. The use of the fish symbol, known as the Ichthys, held great significance for early Christians. It not only symbolized their faith but also conveyed the idea of Christ as the divine Savior. This symbol carried a powerful message of hope and unity for believers in the face of adversity.

Religious iconography played a crucial role in expressing and reinforcing the Christian faith within the catacombs. The use of symbolic imagery allowed early Christians to communicate complex theological concepts in a visual and accessible manner. Furthermore, the presence of these religious symbols served as a shared language among believers. In a time when Christianity faced persecution and was viewed with suspicion by the Roman Empire, these visual representations helped foster a sense of community and unity among Christians. Religious iconography in the catacombs also served as a source of inspiration and encouragement. The depictions of martyrs and saints reminded believers of the ultimate sacrifice made for their faith and encouraged them to persevere in the face of adversity.

Impact of Catacomb Art on Christian Worship

Throughout history, art has held great significance in various aspects of human culture. In the context of Christianity, artistic representations have played a vital role in invoking a sense of devotion and reverence among believers. One particular form of art that has had a profound impact on Christian worship practices is catacomb art. The catacombs, underground burial chambers used by early Christians, served as spaces for both interment and worship. These underground chambers provided a sanctuary for believers to gather and practice their faith in times of persecution. Within the catacombs, various art forms emerged, reflecting the beliefs and values of the early Christian community.

The influence of catacomb art on Christian worship practices can be seen in the way it conveyed important theological concepts, fostered a sense of community, and provided a visual representation of the faith. Many of these artworks depicted scenes from the Bible, such as the miracles of Jesus, the Last Supper, or stories of martyrdom. The impact of catacomb art on Christian worship can be observed through the symbolisms and motifs used in these artworks. For example, the image of the Good Shepherd represented Jesus Christ as the guide and protector of his flock, instilling a sense of comfort and assurance in the hearts of believers. The use of the fish symbol, known as the Ichthys, served as a secret sign of recognition among early Christians and conveyed the message of their faith.

Moreover, catacomb art served as a means of educating and reinforcing Christian beliefs to the illiterate members of the community. Through visual representations, important narratives from the Bible were communicated, allowing individuals to engage with the stories and teachings in a profound way. Artistic representations in the catacombs also played a crucial role in creating a sacred atmosphere conducive to worship. The use of symbols, colors, and imagery evoked a sense of awe and reverence among believers, enhancing their spiritual experience. The very act of descending into the underground catacombs, away from the distractions of the external world, facilitated a deeper connection with God.

Catacomb art has significantly influenced the development of Christian worship practices. Its theological significance, its ability to foster community, and its role in invoking devotion and reverence all contribute to its enduring impact. The artworks found in the catacombs provide a glimpse into the early Christian community's beliefs, values, and devotion to their faith, which continues to inspire and resonate with believers today.

Comparisons with Other Christian Art

Comparison with other forms of art can provide valuable insights into the distinctiveness and significance of catacomb art within the broader artistic tradition. Mosaics and frescoes have long been revered as prominent forms of Christian art, known for their intricate designs and vibrant colors. Mosaics, composed of small pieces of colored glass or stone, were often used to decorate the floors, walls, and ceilings of churches and basilicas. They depicted biblical scenes, saints, and symbols, and were highly regarded for their artistic beauty and religious symbolism.

Frescoes, on the other hand, involved painting directly on wet plaster, allowing the pigments to seep into the wall and become a part of the surface. Churches and religious buildings would often commission frescoes to adorn their interiors, portraying religious narratives or illustrating theological concepts. Frescoes were renowned for their vivid colors and detailed brushwork, creating a sense of life-like realism. While catacomb art shares similarities with mosaics and frescoes in its religious subject matter and symbolism, there are some notable differences that set it apart. Catacombs were underground burial sites for early Christians, and the art found within these burial chambers served a different purpose than the more public and decorative nature of mosaics and frescoes.

Catacomb art often consisted of simple and humble depictions of Christian symbols and stories, carved or painted onto the walls and ceilings of the burial chambers. These images were created by ordinary Christians, conveying their faith and providing solace in times of persecution and hardship. Unlike the grandeur and opulence of mosaics and frescoes, catacomb art reflected the everyday lives and struggles of early Christians. Despite its simplicity, catacomb art played a significant role in the development of Christian iconography and the preservation of Christian history. These underground artworks served as a testimony to the faith and resilience of early Christians, and they also provided a visual means of passing down biblical narratives and teachings.

Furthermore, catacomb art often displayed a distinct Eastern influence, with its use of symbols such as the Chi-Rho, the Good Shepherd, and the fish. These symbols, drawn from the traditions of the

Eastern Mediterranean, reflected the cultural and geographical contexts in which early Christianity thrived. In conclusion, comparing catacomb art with mosaics and frescoes reveals both similarities and distinctive features. While mosaics and frescoes were celebrated for their artistic beauty and grandeur, catacomb art possessed a simplicity and humility that conveyed the everyday faith and struggles of early Christians. These underground artworks served as important visual tools for the preservation of Christian history and the transmission of biblical narratives.

Chapter Eleven

The Influence of Catacomb Art on Christian Worship

Depicting Biblical Stories and Themes in Catacomb Art

The catacombs of ancient Rome offer a unique window into the early Christian world, revealing how believers of the time chose to represent their faith artistically. These subterranean burial places were adorned with art that was rich in biblical narratives and themes. The choice of stories depicted in these underground sanctuaries was not random; they were carefully selected for their theological significance and their ability to offer hope and comfort to the faithful. One prominent theme found in catacomb art is the representation of Christ as the Good Shepherd. This imagery, drawn from passages such as John 10:11-18, resonated deeply with early Christians who saw themselves as part of a flock under Jesus' loving care. The Good Shepherd motif also symbolized Christ's role in leading souls to salvation, an especially poignant message for those mourning the loss of loved ones.

Another recurring subject is the depiction of Old Testament figures like Jonah, Daniel, and Noah—each chosen for their symbolic association with resurrection and deliverance. The story of Jonah, who emerged unharmed from the belly of a great fish after three days, prefigured Christ's own resurrection. Similarly, Daniel's survival in the lions' den and Noah's preservation through the flood were seen as allegories for God's saving grace. These artworks served not only as decoration but also as catechetical tools. In an era when many converts were illiterate, visual representations became a vital means of imparting scriptural knowledge. Frescoes depicting scenes from Jesus' life—his miracles, parables, crucifixion, and resurrection—functioned both as lessons in doctrine and as sources of inspiration. Moreover, catacomb art often included images that conveyed eschatological hope—the promise of eternal life after death. Scenes from revelation or depictions of paradise invited reflection on the ultimate triumph over death through Christ's sacrifice.

In exploring these sacred spaces today, one can sense how early Christians used art to express complex theological ideas and sustain their community's identity amidst persecution. Modern scholars continue to uncover layers of meaning within these ancient frescoes, mosaics, and sculptures—each work contributing to our understanding of early Christian beliefs and practices.

The Use of Catacomb Art in Early Christian Liturgy

Catacomb art played a significant role beyond its immediate visual appeal; it was intricately woven into the fabric of early Christian liturgical practice. As Christianity was not yet fully sanctioned by Roman authorities during much of this period, worship often took place clandestinely within these underground chambers. Herein lies an intimate connection between space, artistry, and ritual that defined early Christian worship experiences. The very act of gathering among the tombs reinforced a sense of communion with those who had passed on—a tangible expression that death did not sever ties within the body of Christ but rather transformed them. This setting provided a powerful backdrop for celebrating the Eucharist or commemorating martyrs' feast days where frescoes bearing witness to faith served both as focal points for meditation and objects that enhanced communal worship.

Artistic representations surrounding worshippers could have functioned pedagogically during liturgies by visually reinforcing spoken words or sung hymns with depictions related directly to scripture readings or doctrinal teachings being shared at that moment. For instance, if a reading pertained to baptismal themes or redemption through water (such as Moses striking water from a rock), nearby images illustrating such events would deepen participants' engagement with the liturgical action unfolding before them. Furthermore, certain symbols recurrently found in catacomb art held particular resonance within liturgical contexts: **anchors** signifying steadfast hope; **doves** representing peace or the Holy Spirit; **breads and fishes** alluding directly to Eucharistic elements; chi-rho monograms pointing towards Christ himself—all these icons served not merely decorative purposes but actively supported worshipers' spiritual contemplation during services.

As we delve deeper into historical records and archaeological findings related to catacombs' use for worship purposes (e.g., inscriptions indicating altars placement), we gain richer insights into how integral these artworks were within formative centuries of Christian liturgy development—a testament indeed to how aesthetics can profoundly shape religious experience itself.

Symbolism and Rituals in Christian Worship

Christianity is replete with symbolism that carries profound meanings for believers—a tradition rooted deeply in its earliest expressions found within catacomb artistry itself. These symbols transcended mere ornamentation; they encapsulated core tenets of faith while simultaneously guiding adherents through various rituals comprising their spiritual lives. One cannot overlook the importance **fish symbol (Ichthys)** which became emblematic of Christianity's secret nature during periods of intense persecution— it stood acrostic Greek phrase "Jesus Christ God Son Savior." Its presence in catacombs reminded faithful covert nature their gatherings also affirmed the central gospel message of salvation through Jesus.

Likewise, **the lamb** is another potent symbol encountered frequently on walls of tombs—an allusion sacrificial Lamb God whose death atoned sins humanity according to biblical narrative thus reinforcing the central aspect of The Communion celebration of the body and blood of Jesus Christ in remembrance of his sacrifice. Rituals themselves imbued deep symbolic significance whether acts of baptism which represented the dying old self rising anew life Christ washing feet humble service to others following the example set by Jesus' Last Supper each gesture performed context worship carried layers of meaning informed by surrounding iconography. Moreover, the

Advent holy day's seasons such as Easter and Pentecost, brought forth specific sets of images and narratives focused on collective memory events that shaped the identity of the community itself thus ensuring the continuity transmission of key beliefs across generations despite external pressures and challenges faced.

In summary, exploration of symbolism rituals inherent in early Christian practice particularly evidenced in artistic output catacombs reveals religion steeped rich tapestry signs gestures each laden meaning purpose every brushstroke chisel mark contributed to the ongoing story of people striving to live out convictions in the midst often hostile world—a narrative continues to unfold present-day global church still finds inspiration roots planted long ago beneath streets ancient Rome.

Chapter Twelve

Legacy of the Christian Catacombs

Influence on Later Christian Art

Exploring the Enduring Influence of Catacomb Art on Later Periods of Christian Art

Within the dark and mysterious catacombs lie hidden treasures that have left an indelible mark on the art of Christianity. The catacomb art, found in the underground burial chambers of early Christians, serves as a testament to their unwavering faith and has had a profound influence on the art that followed. One of the key aspects of catacomb art is its depiction of religious motifs and themes. The artists of the time used simple and symbolic imagery to convey profound spiritual messages. Through their art, they emphasized the hope of resurrection, the triumph of good over evil, and the promise of eternal life.

As later periods of Christian art emerged, the influence of catacomb art became apparent. Artists drew inspiration from these ancient works and incorporated similar motifs and themes into their own creations. This continuity can be seen in the use of the Good Shepherd as a representation of Christ, the depiction of baptism as a symbol of spiritual rebirth, and the portrayal of martyrs as heroic figures. The enduring influence of catacomb art on later Christian art cannot be overstated. It serves as a foundation for artistic expression and provides a connection to the early Christian community. By studying and understanding this art, we gain insights into the beliefs, values, and experiences of those who came before us.

Highlighting the Continuity and Transformation of Artistic Motifs and Religious Themes

Throughout the centuries, the motifs and themes found in catacomb art have undergone a transformation while maintaining a sense of continuity. As Christianity spread and evolved, so too did the artwork that depicted its beliefs and stories. One of the most striking examples of this transformation is the evolution of the image of the fish. In catacomb art, the fish symbolized Christ and his followers. However, as Christianity became the official religion of the Roman Empire, the fish motif became less prominent, giving way to the cross as the primary symbol of Christianity.

Another motif that has endured and evolved is the portrayal of biblical scenes and figures. The catacomb art often depicted scenes from the Old and New Testaments, such as the Last Supper, the miracles of Jesus, and the stories of Adam and Eve. These themes continued to be represented in later Christian art, but with variations and reinterpretations that reflected the cultural and artistic styles of different periods. Furthermore, the religious themes in catacomb art paved the way for the development of Christian iconography. The use of allegorical imagery and symbols in catacomb art laid the foundation for the rich tradition of religious symbolism that can be seen in paintings, sculptures, and stained glass windows throughout history. By highlighting the continuity and transformation of artistic motifs and religious themes, we gain a deeper understanding of the development and significance of Christian art. The art of the catacombs serves as a bridge between the ancient world and the present, reminding us of the enduring power of faith and artistic expression.

Subchapter: Influence on Later Christian Art

The influence of catacomb art on later periods of Christian art is undeniable. Artists looked to the simplicity and symbolism of catacomb art as a source of inspiration and a way to connect with the early Christian community. One of the key ways in which catacomb art influenced later Christian art is through the use of religious symbolism. The artists of the catacombs used simple and easily recognizable symbols to convey profound spiritual messages. These symbols, such as the Chi-Rho, the anchor, and the peacock, continued to be used in later Christian art, serving as visual reminders of the core beliefs and teachings of Christianity.

In addition to symbolism, catacomb art also influenced the portrayal of religious figures. The depictions of Christ, the Virgin Mary, and the saints found in catacomb art set the standard for how these figures were represented in later Christian art. Artists drew inspiration from these early representations, adapting and expanding upon them to create their own unique interpretations. Furthermore, the themes of catacomb art, such as the hope of resurrection and the triumph of good over evil, continued to resonate with later Christian artists. These themes provided a foundation for the exploration of spiritual and theological concepts through art, allowing artists to express their faith and deepen the spiritual experience of viewers.

Overall, the influence of catacomb art on later Christian art is a testament to the enduring power and significance of this ancient form of expression. Through the study and appreciation of catacomb art, we can gain a deeper understanding of the artistic and spiritual traditions that have shaped Christianity throughout history.

Theological Significance

The catacombs, underground burial sites used by early Christians, are a treasure trove of art that offers a unique glimpse into the early Christian faith. The artwork found in these catacombs carries profound theological significance, reflecting the beliefs and practices of the early Christians. Through the study of catacomb art, we can gain a deeper understanding of the theological foundations of Christianity. The art found in the catacombs serves as a visual representation of key theological concepts within Christianity. It not only supports and enhances our understanding of these concepts but also provides historical evidence for the development of Christian beliefs. By analyzing the art in the catacombs, we can draw connections between the images and the theological teachings of the early Church.

Theological Significance:

The catacomb art holds great theological significance, as it offers insights into the early Christian understanding of key theological themes. For example, the depiction of Jesus Christ in the catacomb art highlights the divinity and humanity of Jesus. These depictions often show Jesus as a shepherd, emphasizing his role as the Good Shepherd who guides and protects his flock. Furthermore, catacomb art often depicts scenes from the Old Testament, such as the story of Jonah and the whale or Daniel in the lion's den. By including these biblical stories in their artwork, the early Christians were emphasizing the continuity between the Old Testament and the teachings of Jesus Christ. This reinforces the idea that Christianity is rooted in the promises and prophecies of the Old Testament.

The art also serves as a powerful tool for communicating theological concepts to illiterate Christians. In a time when the majority of the population was unable to read, the visual nature of the art allowed people to understand and engage with theological ideas in a tangible way. The catacomb art thus played a crucial role in the transmission of Christian teachings. Additionally, the catacomb art often depicts scenes of martyrdom, showcasing the courage and faith of those who died for their beliefs. These images serve as a reminder of the sacrifices made by early Christians and inspire present-day believers to remain steadfast in their faith.

Overall, the catacomb art carries immense theological significance. It reveals the early Christian understanding of Jesus Christ, the connection between the Old and New Testaments, and the importance of martyrdom. By studying and appreciating the art of the catacombs, we can gain a deeper appreciation for the theological foundations of the Christian faith.

Contemporary Interest in Catacomb Art

- Catacomb art has gained significant attention in contemporary society due to its unique historical and artistic value.

- Many individuals, particularly those interested in art, Christian apologetics, and Christian history, have been captivated by the intricate and symbolic artwork found within the catacombs.

- One of the reasons for this ongoing fascination is the mystery that surrounds the creation of these artworks, as well as the stories they tell about the early Christian community.

- The depth and complexity of the imagery found in catacomb art have attracted scholars, artists, and enthusiasts, sparking further exploration and interpretation of these hidden treasures.

- Through examining and appreciating catacomb art, contemporary society gains a deeper understanding of the historical context, cultural practices, and religious beliefs of early Christians.

- The fascination with catacomb art extends beyond mere aesthetics, as it provides valuable insights into the world of early Christianity.

- By studying the iconography and symbols present in catacomb art, historians and archaeologists can reconstruct a more complete picture of the beliefs, rituals, and social dynamics of early Christian communities.

- Catacomb art also sheds light on the challenges and struggles faced by early Christians, particularly during times of persecution.

- Through analyzing the artistic choices and motifs found in catacomb art, scholars can uncover hidden meanings and messages that were often encoded to communicate Christian faith and identity in a covert manner.

- Furthermore, the preservation of catacomb art allows contemporary society to appreciate the rich cultural heritage of early Christianity and fosters a sense of connection to the past.

- By understanding and valuing catacomb art, individuals can engage with the history and culture of Christianity in a more profound and meaningful way.

Persecution and Resistance through Art

During times of persecution, catacomb art played a significant role in expressing resistance and resilience. These underground burial sites, used mainly by early Christians, provided a space for artistic expression that served as both silent protest and affirmation of their Christian identity. The art found in the catacombs served as a powerful form of resistance against the persecution faced by Christians. It was a way for them to assert their beliefs and identity in the face of adversity. The art often depicted biblical scenes and symbols that held special meaning for Christians, such as the Good Shepherd and the fish symbol. These images served as a reminder of their faith and provided solace in challenging times.

One of the subversive aspects of catacomb art was its hidden nature. The catacombs were hidden underground, and the art was often created in hidden corners and passageways. This hiddenness allowed Christians to express their faith in secret, away from the prying eyes of their persecutors. The art became a way to communicate their beliefs and to connect with other believers without drawing unwanted attention. Additionally, catacomb art served as a form of silent protest against the oppressive Roman regime. By creating and displaying Christian imagery in this clandestine environment, early Christians were subtly asserting their defiance and refusal to conform to the pagan practices and beliefs of the empire. This art served as a powerful statement of their nonconformity and resistance. It is important to note that catacomb art not only expressed resistance but also served as a source of hope and inspiration for persecuted Christians. The art depicted scenes of martyrdom, showing believers who had been faithful to their beliefs until death. These depictions served as a reminder of the strength and courage displayed by those who came before them and served as a source of encouragement to continue in their own faith.

In summary, catacomb art played a crucial role in expressing resistance and resilience during times of persecution. It served as a form of silent protest and affirmation of Christian identity, allowing believers to express their faith in secret and assert their defiance against the oppressive regime. The art provided hope and inspiration to persecuted Christians, reminding them of the strength and courage shown by those who had gone before them.

The Influence of Catacomb Art on Christian Worship

Throughout history, art has played a significant role not only in the expression of human creativity but also in shaping religious practices and beliefs. The catacombs, underground burial sites used by early Christians, hold a wealth of artistic representations that provide insights into the development of liturgical practices and sacred spaces. One of the key ways in which catacomb art influenced Christian worship was through its depictions of biblical scenes and religious symbols. These paintings and sculptures served as visual aids, helping illiterate or less educated worshipers understand and connect with the stories and teachings of the Bible. The art served as a form of religious instruction, inviting believers to reflect on the significance of the depicted events and characters.

Furthermore, catacomb art played a crucial role in fostering a sense of community and belonging among early Christians. The images and symbols portrayed in the catacombs reinforced the shared faith and values of the community, creating a visual language that united believers in their worship practices. These artistic representations provided a source of comfort, encouragement, and inspiration for individuals facing persecution and hardships. The catacombs also served as sacred spaces where worshipers could gather to pray and commemorate their faith. The art adorning the walls and tombs created an atmosphere of reverence and awe, encouraging worshipers to engage in contemplative and reflective practices. The dimly lit passages, adorned with symbolic imagery, created an otherworldly ambiance that heightened the spiritual experience of those who entered.

Catacomb art had a profound influence on the development of liturgical practices and the shaping of sacred spaces. Its visual representations aided in the dissemination of religious knowledge and fostered a sense of community among early Christians. The art created an environment conducive to worship, inviting believers to connect with their faith on a deeper level. Through the study of catacomb art, we gain valuable insights into the religious experiences of worshipers in the early Christian era.

The Evolution of Christian Iconography in the Catacombs

From Simple Symbols to Elaborate Imagery: The Development of Iconography

The evolution of Christian iconography within the catacombs is a fascinating journey from simplicity to complexity. Initially, early Christians used discreet symbols to identify and express their faith. These symbols included **the ichthys (fish),** which represented Jesus Christ; **the anchor**, symbolizing hope; and **the chi-rho**, an emblem formed by superimposing the first two letters of 'Christ' in Greek. As Christianity grew and became more accepted within Roman society, these simple symbols evolved into more elaborate and narrative-driven imagery.

This progression can be seen in the depiction of biblical stories that began to adorn the walls of catacombs. Scenes such as Daniel in the lion's den, Jonah being swallowed by a great fish, and Noah in his ark were not only illustrations of faith but also served as allegories for resurrection and salvation—central themes for those buried within these subterranean burial places. Moreover, portraiture became prevalent with images of Christ as **the Good Shepherd** or **Pantocrator** (Ruler of All) emerging during this period. This shift towards more complex iconography was partly due to increased artistic skill among Christian artists but also reflected a growing confidence within the community to openly display their beliefs. The development of iconography was not uniform across all regions or communities. In some areas, particularly where persecution was still rife, simpler symbols persisted longer. However, over time even these communities began adopting more detailed representations as part of their devotional practices.

Influences from Greco-Roman and Jewish Traditions on Christian Iconography

Christian iconography did not develop in isolation but was significantly influenced by existing Greco-Roman and Jewish artistic traditions. Early Christians lived in a world rich with visual symbolism from various religious backgrounds, which they adapted for their own purposes. Greco-Roman influences are evident in stylistic elements such as composition, perspective, and use of color found in catacomb art. For instance, depictions of Christ often borrowed from portrayals of Apollo or Orpheus—figures who were associated with life-giving powers similar to those attributed to Jesus. Additionally, funerary motifs common in Roman art were reinterpreted with Christian significance; sarcophagi adorned with vines spoke not just of earthly life but eternal life in Christ. Jewish traditions also played a role in shaping early Christian imagery.

Many early Christians were Jews or familiar with Jewish customs and scriptures. As such, they incorporated elements like menorahs or representations from Hebrew scripture into their art forms. The story of Jonah was particularly significant because it prefigured Jesus' resurrection after three days—a central tenet for both Jews anticipating deliverance and Christians affirming Christ's triumph over death. These cultural exchanges led to a unique blend within Christian art that allowed believers to connect their new faith with familiar visual languages while simultaneously distinguishing themselves from other religious groups.

The Spread of Iconographic Styles across Different Regions

As Christianity spread throughout different regions of the Roman Empire—and eventually beyond—so too did its iconographic styles evolve uniquely within each locale. While certain core themes remained consistent due to shared theological beliefs (such as resurrection), local cultures influenced how these themes were artistically expressed. In Rome itself, where many catacombs are located, there was an emphasis on grandeur reflective of imperial power structures—even though Christians often faced persecution there. This resulted in majestic portrayals like Christ enthroned amidst apostles or saints depicted with halos signifying holiness akin to Roman depictions of divine figures.

Moving eastward towards Byzantium (modern-day Istanbul), one observes an increasing sophistication and stylization characteristic of what would become known as Byzantine art—a style that would dominate Eastern Christianity for centuries. Here icons took on a spiritual quality through elongated figures and ethereal golden backgrounds emphasizing divinity over earthly realism. Conversely, Coptic Christian communities in Egypt integrated indigenous artistic conventions into their religious artwork resulting in distinctive expressions that differed markedly from those found elsewhere around the Mediterranean basin. Throughout this diffusion process across different regions emerged localized schools where artists developed specific techniques or thematic focuses reflecting both universal aspects of Christianity and particular cultural identities—demonstrating how deeply intertwined religion can become with cultural expression even when sharing common roots.

Chapter Fourteen

Miracles and Healing Depicted in Catacomb Art

Miraculous Healing as a Theme in Early Christian Artwork

The early Christian community, emerging within the Roman Empire, faced numerous challenges and adversities. In this context, miraculous healings served not only as a testament to divine intervention but also as a source of hope and affirmation for believers. The theme of miraculous healings in early Christian artwork is a reflection of this deep-seated belief in the power of faith to transcend earthly suffering. Artwork from this period often depicted scenes from the New Testament, where Jesus performed miracles that healed the sick and infirm. These images served multiple purposes: they were didactic, teaching the stories of Christianity; they were inspirational, offering comfort to those who were suffering; and they were apologetic, providing evidence of Christ's divinity and thus legitimizing the Christian faith amidst a pagan world.

In exploring these artworks further, one can see that artists chose specific miracles that resonated with their communities. For instance, the healing of the paralytic underscored Jesus' authority over physical ailments and was particularly poignant for those seeking relief from their own afflictions. Similarly, depictions of Christ restoring sight to the blind could be interpreted metaphorically—Christ enlightening not just physical vision but also spiritual insight. Moreover, these artworks often employed symbolic elements to convey deeper meanings. The use of light around Christ's figure in such scenes symbolized divine presence and purity. The gestures and expressions of figures receiving healing emphasized humility and faith—a message to viewers about the proper attitude towards divine grace.

The catacombs themselves provided an intimate setting for these artworks. As subterranean burial places for Christians, they were sanctuaries from Roman persecution where believers could freely express their faith through art. Here, miraculous healings depicted on frescoes or carved into sarcophagi reinforced communal beliefs while serving as visual sermons for those who visited these sacred spaces.

Depictions of Jesus' Miracles in the Catacombs

The catacombs are an extensive network of underground burial chambers used by early Christians in Rome. Within these solemn corridors adorned with art lies a rich tapestry depicting various miracles performed by Jesus Christ—each chosen carefully for its significance to early Christian theology and practice. One notable example is found in the **Catacomb of Priscilla** where frescoes illustrate scenes such as

Jesus raising Lazarus from the dead—a powerful symbol of resurrection and eternal life that resonated deeply with those burying their loved ones amidst hopes for an afterlife.

Another significant depiction is that of Jesus multiplying loaves and fishes—an image found in several catacombs including those of San Callisto and Domitilla. This miracle was especially meaningful because it prefigured the Eucharist—a central sacrament in Christianity symbolizing spiritual nourishment and community unity. These depictions are characterized by simplicity yet profound symbolism; they lack elaborate backgrounds or extraneous details common in later religious art. Instead, focus is placed on interactions between Christ and those he heals or helps—emphasizing personal connection with divinity rather than grandeur or opulence. Furthermore, some scholars suggest that certain iconography within these images may have served as coded messages during times when Christianity was not fully sanctioned by Roman authorities. For instance, fish imagery associated with Christ (ichthys) was both a reference to his miracles involving fish but also an acronym for "Jesus Christ God's Son Savior," serving as a discreet signifier among believers.

Healing Shrines and Pilgrimage Sites Associated with Catacombs

Beyond being mere repositories for the dead or canvases for religious expression, some catacombs became associated with healing shrines or pilgrimage sites due to their connection with martyrs or saints reputed to have healing powers interceding on behalf of supplicants. For example, at the Catacomb of Saint Sebastian along Via Appia Antica—one such site—pilgrims would gather seeking cures or solace through prayer near relics believed imbued with holy potency derived from Saint Sebastian himself who suffered martyrdom during Emperor Diocletian's reign but whose intercession was sought after due to his steadfast faith under torture. Additionally, veneration at these sites often included rituals like touching reliquaries containing bones or other remains—or even lying atop graves— in hopes that proximity might facilitate divine intervention leading to miraculous cures much like those depicted on surrounding walls illustrating biblical precedents set forth by Jesus' own acts upon earth centuries prior.

Over time some catacomb sites evolved into more formalized centers for pilgrimage complete with chapels above ground built specifically for worshipers traveling great distances drawn by accounts circulating within hagiographies extolling virtues attributed thereto such saints' efficacious intercessory capabilities regarding health-related issues among faithful adherents seeking aid beyond mere mortal means available at hand during antiquity's latter days transitioning slowly towards medieval era's dawn ahead still shrouded then within mists veiling future unfolding gradually across Europe's broad expanse beneath Christianity's ever-widening embrace enveloping continent whole eventually over ensuing centuries long since past now into history's vast oceanic depths receding far behind us today looking retrospectively across time's wide chasm separating us here now from there then so very far away yet somehow still connected through shared human experience transcending temporal boundaries binding us all together across ages immemorial unto eternity itself everlasting unbroken chain linking every generation one unto another forevermore without end amen.

Chapter Fifteen

Funerary Practices and Burial Rites Reflected in Catacomb Art

Funeral Processions and Mourning Scenes in Early Christian Artwork The catacombs of ancient Rome offer a unique window into the funerary practices and beliefs of early Christians. Within these subterranean burial sites, the artwork adorning the walls provides poignant insights into how early Christians viewed death and the afterlife. Funeral processions and mourning scenes are recurring motifs in this chart, serving as both a testament to the communal nature of grief and a reflection of religious conviction. One can observe in these artworks that funeral processions were not merely about transporting the deceased to their final resting place; they were also ceremonial acts that involved the community. The imagery often depicts groups of figures, sometimes including family members and clergy, accompanying the bier or sarcophagus. These scenes emphasize solidarity among believers in times of loss, illustrating how death was approached with collective support rather than isolation.

Mourning scenes within catacomb art are particularly evocative. They frequently show individuals in gestures of lamentation—raising their hands towards heaven or bowing their heads in sorrow. Such depictions resonate with biblical expressions of mourning but also serve to remind viewers of the hope for resurrection. In some instances, these scenes include symbolic elements such as doves or olive branches, which suggest peace and spiritual transcendence beyond earthly suffering. These artworks also reveal cultural influences from Roman funerary traditions while simultaneously distinguishing themselves through distinct Christian iconography. For example, while Roman art might celebrate the deceased's earthly achievements, Christian art focuses on spiritual virtues and promises of eternal life.

In examining specific examples like the frescoes from the Catacomb of Callixtus, one can discern an evolution in style and symbolism over time. Early images may be simple and symbolic, while later ones become more narrative-driven, possibly reflecting theological developments or changes in liturgical practices.

Symbolism of Death, Resurrection, and Eternal Life in Catacomb Art

Catacomb art is rich with symbols that convey complex theological concepts concerning death, resurrection, and eternal life. This visual language served to reinforce faith among believers during times when Christianity was still developing its doctrines—and often under persecution. The most pervasive symbol found within these underground galleries is that of **the Good Shepherd**. Modeled after pagan representations yet imbued with new meaning by Christians, it illustrates Christ's role as protector and guide to eternal life. The shepherd is often shown carrying a sheep on his shoulders—a direct reference to Jesus' parable about leaving ninety-nine sheep to find one that is lost (Luke 15:4-7), which resonated deeply with notions of salvation.

Another common motif is that of **Jonah being swallowed by a great fish**— only to be delivered safely three days later—a story interpreted by early Christians as prefiguring Christ's resurrection after three days in the tomb. This image served as a powerful reminder that death was not an end but a passage to new life through Christ's triumph over death. Additionally, catacomb art features an abundance of vine imagery which alludes to passages from John 15 where Jesus describes himself as "the true vine." Believers are depicted as branches drawing sustenance from Christ—the source of eternal life—emphasizing their connection to him even beyond death.

The peacock is another symbol encountered within catacomb paintings; its flesh was believed not to decay after death—analogous to Christian beliefs about immortality. Similarly, phoenix imagery speaks directly to themes of rebirth and immortality central to Christian eschatology. These symbols were not only meant for doctrinal instruction but also provided comfort for those grieving loved ones by offering assurance about their fate after death—a fate characterized by reunion with God rather than oblivion or endless wandering in Hades as per pagan beliefs.

Inscriptions, Epitaphs, and Personalization on Funerary Art

The personalization found on funerary art within catacombs reveals much about individual lives within early Christian communities—as well as broader social dynamics at play during this formative period for Christianity. Inscriptions serve multiple purposes: they identify who lies buried within a particular niche; they offer prayers or blessings upon the deceased; they express grief or hope; sometimes they even provide brief biographical details such as occupation or familial relationships. These epitaphs thus create intimate connections between past individuals' lives and present-day observers exploring these ancient spaces. A notable aspect is how inscriptions reflect egalitarian principles espoused by Christianity at this time—slaves could be commemorated with similar dignity afforded free persons or even nobility. This practice contrasts sharply with Roman societal norms where status dictated commemoration quality post-mortem. Moreover, epitaphs occasionally contain scriptural references tailored specifically for those interred—suggesting personalized pastoral care extended even unto deathbeds or funeral rites themselves. For instance, phrases like "in peace" echo New Testament assurances regarding peaceful repose awaiting faithful souls (Luke 2:29).

Artistic personalization goes beyond mere text; portraits integrated into wall paintings now feature faces that were once connected to names, now immortalized on stone tablets nearby. This practice humanizes anonymous remains scattered throughout the labyrinthine corridors beneath Rome's streets. This holds true today, just as it did over two millennia ago when they were first laid to rest beneath the bustling city above. Despite being unseen below the surface then and now, the connection remains unchanged across the ages. It spans the gap between our time and theirs, bridging the history of humanity with a shared commonality, regardless of the era in which we live and eventually pass away.

This unbroken chain of destiny links generations, past and future, creating a shared heritage. We are born, live, die, and return to the same earth from which we originated, only to begin anew in an eternal cycle. With each passing generation, the footsteps of those who came before us pave the way, forming a complete journey that endlessly repeats. In each cycle, we leave behind a legacy, remembered fondly by those who come after us. As we depart, the echoes of our existence resonate through eternity, creating a lasting impact that is still felt today.

In humble tombs, the stories of lives lived, love, lost, and the marks left on the world are preserved for eternity. These small measures contribute to the perpetual memory of our existence. In this way, the scene is set, and the stage is left for others to take their place, continuing the story that began so long ago. It unfolds day by day, year by year, century by century, millennium by millennium, onward to infinity without end. Amen.

Chapter Sixteen

The Influence of Roman Mythology on Christian Iconography

Incorporating Roman Mythological Figures into Christian Art

The incorporation of Roman mythological figures into Christian art is a complex phenomenon that reflects the dynamic cultural exchanges between pagan and Christian traditions during the early centuries of Christianity. This process can be viewed through two lenses: adaptation, where elements sints are adjusted to fit a new context, and appropriation, where they are taken over, sometimes without acknowledgment of their original significance. In the early days of

Christianity, converts often came from diverse backgrounds, bringing with them their cultural and religious symbols. As a result, Christian artists began to adapt these familiar motifs to convey Christian narratives. For instance, the image of Orpheus taming wild animals with his music was reinterpreted as Christ pacifying the souls with his divine message. The Good Shepherd motif is another example; it was an established icon in pagan art that Christians adapted to represent Christ caring for his flock.

However, this process raises questions about whether such use of pagan imagery constitutes appropriation. Some scholars argue that by co-opting these figures without fully acknowledging their origins or altering their meanings significantly, early Christians obscured the original mythological context in favor of promoting their own religious agenda. Moreover, this blending wasn't merely artistic but also theological. Early Church Fathers like Clement of Alexandria advocated for the "spoiling of the Egyptians," suggesting that Christians should adopt non-Christian wisdom if it could be used for a godly purpose. This approach led to a selective integration where certain attributes of Roman deities were assimilated into depictions of saints and angels while maintaining a clear distinction from their polytheistic roots.

An example is the depiction of Fortuna, the goddess of fortune and luck, whose iconography influenced representations of Tyche in Byzantine art and later personifications such as Lady Luck in Western culture. In Christian contexts, however, her wheel became associated with the notion of divine providence rather than random fate. This nuanced interplay between adaptation and appropriation reveals how early Christians navigated their relationship with surrounding cultures— adopting what was useful or attractive while reshaping it within a monotheistic framework that rejected polytheism's core tenets.

Transforming Pagan Symbols into Christian Symbols

The transformation process from pagan symbols to Christian ones represents not just an aesthetic shift but also a profound recontextualization of meaning. Early Christians lived in an environment steeped in Roman mythology and symbolism; thus, they sought ways to express their faith using familiar visual language while infusing it with new significance. One prominent example is the conversion of Sol Invictus (the Unconquered Sun), whose imagery influenced representations of Christ as "the light of the world." The halo seen around Christ's head in many pieces of art has its origins in solar iconography associated with sun gods like Helios or Apollo. By adopting this symbol, Christians could visually express divinity and holiness while simultaneously distancing themselves from idolatrous worship.

Another significant transformation occurred with architectural structures like temples and basilicas. While originally designed for pagan worship or public affairs respectively, these buildings were repurposed by Christians for worship spaces—basilicas becoming particularly important as prototypes for church architecture. Symbols such as laurel wreaths underwent similar reinterpretations; once indicative of victory or imperial authority within Roman culture, they came to symbolize martyrdom's triumph over death within Christianity. The cross itself—a tool for execution—was transformed into a symbol representing salvation and eternal life through Jesus' crucifixion and resurrection narrative. These transformations were not always straightforward or universally accepted among early Christians; some resisted incorporating any formative elements from paganism due to concerns about syncretism—the blending or amalgamation which might dilute pure doctrine. Nevertheless, over time these symbols became so entrenched within Christian iconography that their pagan origins faded from collective memory.

Exploring the Interplay between Roman Mythology and Christianity

The connection between Roman mythology and Christianity can be described through the concepts of syncretism, where distinct beliefs blend, and synthesis, a deliberate combination that creates something new while preserving individual identities. Early Christianity emerged in a diverse society with rich religious traditions, leading to inevitable interactions between different belief systems. Syncretism occurred as converts brought practices from previous religions, seamlessly integrating them into Christian rituals. This included celebrating certain feast days on dates once dedicated to pagan gods and adopting local customs related to sacred spaces.

Conscious synthesis was also evident, particularly among theologians who aimed to express faith using philosophical terms borrowed from Hellenistic thought. This thought had already assimilated aspects from various mythologies, including those under Rome's influence. Justin Martyr, for example, argued that seeds of truth existed in all cultures, prefiguring full revelation through Christ, emphasizing an inclusive perspective on knowledge beyond Judeo-Christian sources. This synthesis extended beyond theology into visual arts, literature, and liturgy, illustrating the deep integration of Greco-Roman culture into everyday life, even among believers striving to maintain a distinct identity in the face of persecution and the official religion of the Roman Empire.

Despite the eventual tolerance granted by Constantine's conversion and the Edict of Milan in 313 CE, which allowed freedom of religion, tensions persisted. Periodic purges against perceived remnants of paganism within church practices and debates regarding the appropriateness of venerating saints and relics reflected ongoing struggles. Some viewed such practices as dangerously close to the idolatry of ancient Romans.

In conclusion, an examination of the influence of Roman mythology on Christian iconography reveals a multifaceted interaction, encompassing subtle adaptations and outright appropriations. This interaction has resulted in a complex tapestry of symbols and narratives that define much of Western spiritual and artistic heritage today. These interactions still provoke discussions about boundaries, authenticity in religious expression, and the preservation of cultural heritage amid the ongoing evolution of beliefs and ideas in our globalized world.

Chapter Seventeen

The Spread of Christianity and Catacomb Art in the Late Antique Period

Catacombs Beyond Rome: Christian Burial Sites in Other Regions While the catacombs of Rome are the most famous, the practice of burying the dead in underground chambers spread throughout the Roman Empire as Christianity took root in various regions. In places like Naples, Sicily, North Africa, and even as far as Alexandria in Egypt, early Christians adopted similar burial practices. These catacombs were not mere carbon copies of their Roman counterparts; they reflected local customs, geology, and artistic influences. In Naples, for example, the Catacombs of San Gennaro display a blend of pagan and Christian imagery that speaks to a community transitioning between old and new beliefs. The frescoes here are vibrant with depictions of biblical scenes alongside traditional Roman motifs. Similarly, in Sicily's Catacombs of St. John in Syracuse, one can observe a unique intermingling of Greek and Christian art traditions.

North Africa presents another fascinating case study with its own distinct catacomb art. The region's strong ties to both Rome and indigenous Berber culture resulted in burial chambers that were less elaborate than those found in Rome but rich with symbolic artwork such as peacocks representing immortality and olive branches signifying peace. Alexandria's catacombs reveal an even more diverse cultural mix due to Egypt's position as a crossroads between Africa and Asia. The Catacomb of Kom el Shoqafa is particularly noteworthy for its fusion of Pharaonic motifs, Greco-Roman artistry, and emerging Christian symbols—a testament to Alexandria's cosmopolitan nature during Late Antiquity. These regional variations not only demonstrate the adaptability of Christian burial practices but also highlight how early Christians expressed their faith within different cultural contexts while maintaining core religious themes across disparate geographies.

Regional Variations in Catacomb Art Styles

The art found within catacombs across different regions tells a story not just of religious belief but also of cultural exchange and adaptation. While some elements remained consistent—such as the use of the Good Shepherd or Orant figures—there was considerable variation influenced by local traditions and available materials. In Rome itself, there was an evolution from simple decoration towards more sophisticated narrative scenes from scripture by the 4th century. This trend mirrored broader developments within Roman art but was infused with distinctly Christian symbolism.

Moving away from Rome to areas like Dalmatia (modern-day Croatia), we find simpler frescoes yet ones that still convey powerful spiritual messages through symbols such as bread and fish or anchors representing hope. These artworks often had less detail due to limited resources or perhaps because these communities placed greater emphasis on symbolic meaning over artistic flourish. In contrast, Eastern regions under Byzantine influence developed a style characterized by more rigid iconography reflecting theological debates about Christ's nature that were central to Eastern Christianity at this time. Here we see a greater use of gold backgrounds and iconic representations which would later become hallmarks of Byzantine art.

The Iberian Peninsula offers another intriguing case where Visigothic rule introduced Germanic elements into local Christian art. This amalgamation resulted in distinctive architectural features such as horseshoe arches being incorporated into tomb structures along with frescoes that bore both Visigothic geometric patterns and traditional Christian imagery. Each region's catacomb art thus serves as an archaeological record not only for understanding early Christianity but also for tracing how it intersected with other cultures during its expansion across Europe and beyond.

The Impact of Constantine's Conversion on Christian Art and Worship

Constantine's conversion to Christianity marked a turning point not only for the religion itself but also for its artistic expression. With imperial support came legitimacy—and resources—that transformed how Christians worshipped and depicted their faith. Before Constantine's Edict of Milan in 313 AD granted tolerance to Christianity within the empire, much Christian worship had been clandestine due to persecution. Post-conversion however saw an unprecedented construction boom for churches across the empire which necessitated new forms of religious art on a scale previously unimaginable for this once-underground faith.

This period witnessed the rise of grand basilicas adorned with mosaics depicting biblical narratives designed both to educate illiterate congregants about scripture stories and reinforce doctrinal messages amidst ongoing theological disputes about Christ's divinity among other issues facing an increasingly diverse church body. Christian iconography became standardized during this time; symbols like chi-rho (□), representing Christ's name became ubiquitous throughout Christendom thanks largely to Constantine's patronage who used it on his military standard—the Labarum—as well as his coinage thereby disseminating these images widely throughout his realm reinforcing his commitment to his newfound faith publicly.

Moreover, Constantine's reign saw significant developments in liturgical furnishings such as altars which now needed to be visually impressive given their central role within larger worship spaces compared to earlier house churches where communion might have been celebrated on simple wooden tables without much adornment if any at all given constraints imposed by secrecy prior state recognition acceptance Christianity officially sanctioned religion Empire-wide following Constantinople founding 330 AD onwards leading further enhancements ecclesiastical architecture and decorative arts alike setting the stage medieval period followed thereafter fundamentally altering the trajectory Western civilization process laying the foundations what would eventually become known today as modern Europe culturally speaking least partly thanks large measure impact Constantine's conversion had upon world history general specifically regards development subsequent proliferation early medieval era onwards until present day times inclusive thereof.

Chapter Eighteen

The Legacy of Catacomb Art in Later Christian Art Movements

Influence on Byzantine Iconography and Mosaics

The catacombs of early Christianity, with their rich tapestry of art, served as a foundational bedrock for the development of later Christian artistic traditions, including the Byzantine iconography and mosaics that flourished from the 4th century onward. The visual language developed in the dimly lit corridors beneath Rome provided a lexicon of symbols and narratives that would be translated into the opulent and expressive art of the Byzantine Empire. Byzantine iconography owes much to these early Christian images. The catacomb paintings often depicted biblical scenes and figures with an emphasis on spiritual significance rather than physical realism. This approach resonated with Byzantine artists who sought to convey theological truths over mimetic representation. Icons, therefore, became windows to heaven, focusing on conveying divine presence through stylized features such as large, penetrating eyes and elongated figures.

Mosaics in churches like Hagia Sophia in Constantinople (modern-day Istanbul) demonstrate a direct lineage from catacomb art in their use of symbolic imagery. The gold backgrounds seen in many Byzantine mosaics echo the otherworldly atmospheres suggested by the luminous halos found around figures in catacomb frescoes. Moreover, themes popular in catacomb art, such as Christ as the Good Shepherd or Orants (praying figures), were adapted into grander scales within basilicas across the empire.

The transition from hidden worship spaces to grand public structures did not diminish the importance of these early artworks; instead, it amplified their influence. As Christianity became more accepted and eventually state- sponsored under Emperor Constantine and his successors, artists had greater freedom to expand upon these motifs within public religious spaces. Furthermore, techniques used by artists in catacombs—such as fresco painting—were refined and adapted for larger-scale works seen throughout Byzantium. The process of creating mosaics also evolved but maintained its roots in arranging small pieces to create a cohesive narrative image—a concept not dissimilar to piecing together symbolic representations within cramped burial niches.

Revival of Interest in Catacomb Art during the Renaissance
During the Renaissance—a period marked by a resurgence of interest in classical antiquity—scholars and artists rediscovered ancient

texts and artifacts that had been lost or neglected during previous centuries. This revival extended to early Christian art found within Rome's catacombs when they were systematically explored starting from the late 16th century onwards. Renaissance humanists saw themselves as intellectual heirs to both classical Rome and early Christianity; thus, they were fascinated by catacomb art which bridged these worlds through its synthesis of Roman artistic techniques with Christian themes. Artists like Michelangelo Buonarroti studied ancient Roman frescoes which influenced his work on the Sistine Chapel ceiling where he incorporated robust physical forms derived from classical sculpture alongside Christian iconography reminiscent of those found underground.

Moreover, this period saw an increased focus on historical accuracy—or at least an idealized version thereof—in depicting biblical events. Catacomb art offered authentic templates for portraying early Christians which appealed greatly to Renaissance sensibilities about reviving antiquity's glory days. Artists such as Raphael took inspiration from these primitive Christians' expressions of faith when designing his own ecclesiastical commissions like 'The Liberation of Saint Peter' in Vatican's Stanza di Eliodoro where he employed dramatic lighting effects similar to those experienced within subterranean chapels. Additionally, archaeological interest led to preservation efforts aimed at restoring damaged frescoes within catacombs—an endeavor that paralleled broader conservation activities undertaken during this era for other ancient artworks deemed culturally significant.

Contemporary Artists Inspired by the Aesthetics and Themes of Catacomb Art

In contemporary times, there has been a renewed fascination with early Christian catacomb art among modern artists who find resonance with its themes of mortality, transcendence, and communal identity—all increasingly relevant in today's globalized yet fragmented world. Artists like Bill Viola have drawn upon both thematic elements—the existential ponderings—and stylistic cues—the ethereal ambiance—from catacomb paintings for their video installations which often explore human experiences such as birth, death, suffering, and redemption. Viola's works are immersive experiences that echo both form (the enveloping nature of being inside a tomb) and content (the spiritual reflections prompted by mortality).

Similarly inspired is El Mac whose murals frequently incorporate haloed figures reminiscent of saints depicted within ancient Christian tombs but recontextualized against urban landscapes thus creating dialogues between past faith expressions and contemporary social realities. Moreover, some contemporary religious communities have looked back towards these earliest expressions of their faith tradition for inspiration when commissioning new works for places of worship or meditation spaces— seeking simplicity amid complexity much like their forebears did beneath Roman soil centuries ago. These modern interpretations do not merely replicate old styles but engage them critically—asking what it means to express spirituality through art today while acknowledging a lineage stretching back through darkened tunnels lined with stories told through paint upon stone.

Chapter Nineteen

Interpreting and Understanding Catacomb Art Today

Challenges and Controversies in Interpreting Catacomb Artwork Interpreting catacomb artwork presents a unique set of challenges and controversies that stem from the complex interplay between art, history, and religion. One of the primary difficulties is the lack of written records accompanying these artworks. Unlike other historical artifacts, catacomb paintings and sculptures rarely come with explanations or descriptions, leaving their interpretation open to scholarly debate. The ambiguity of symbols is another significant challenge. Early Christian iconography often borrowed elements from contemporary pagan culture, leading to a syncretism that can be difficult to unravel. For instance, the image of a shepherd could represent Christ as "the Good Shepherd," but it could also be an adaptation of the pagan figure Orpheus or even a symbol of philanthropy without specific religious connotations. Moreover, there's the issue of anachronistic interpretations—modern viewers may project contemporary understandings onto ancient images, distorting their original meaning. Scholars must resist reading later doctrinal developments back into these early works, which were created in a period when Christian theology was not yet fully codified.

Controversies also arise over the purpose and context of these artworks. Some argue that they were meant to convey theological messages or serve as tools for catechesis among early Christians. Others suggest they primarily fulfilled a decorative function or served to assert identity and continuity in times of persecution. Furthermore, restoration practices have sometimes led to debates about authenticity and historical accuracy. Restorations done with good intentions have occasionally altered original features or introduced modern materials that change our perception of the artwork's original state. To navigate these challenges, scholars employ interdisciplinary approaches combining art history, theology, archaeology, and philology. They also rely on comparative studies with contemporary art forms from different cultures and regions to better understand the unique characteristics of catacomb art.

Using Technology to Enhance Analysis and Interpretation

Technological advancements have revolutionized how we analyze and interpret catacomb art today. Non-invasive imaging techniques like infrared photography can reveal underdrawings or faded pigments invisible to the naked eye. This allows researchers to understand better the artists' methods and intentions without damaging fragile artworks. Digital reconstruction has become an invaluable tool for visualizing how catacombs originally appeared. By creating 3D models based on laser scans or photogrammetry data, experts can simulate lighting conditions, architectural structures, and placement of artworks within their spatial context—providing insights into how these spaces were experienced by ancient visitors.

Another area where technology aids interpretation is through pigment analysis using spectroscopy or X-ray fluorescence (XRF). These methods help identify the materials used by artists—information that can shed light on trade routes, technological capabilities, and socio-economic conditions at the time. Moreover, databases compiling photographs, descriptions, and scholarly literature on catacomb art facilitate cross-referencing between sites scattered across different regions. This interconnectedness helps scholars detect patterns in iconography or stylistic developments over time. Technology also plays a role in preserving these delicate artworks for future generations through digital archiving initiatives that create high-resolution records before further deterioration occurs due to environmental factors or human interference. However impressive these technological tools are though; they cannot replace human expertise entirely. The nuanced understanding required for interpreting symbolic content still relies heavily on scholarly insight grounded in deep knowledge of historical contexts.

The Importance of Contextualizing Catacomb Art within Historical, Social, and Religious Frameworks To fully appreciate catacomb art's significance requires placing it within its broader historical narrative—a narrative marked by social upheaval and religious transformation during late antiquity. The Roman Empire's shifting political landscape profoundly influenced early Christian communities' lives—and by extension—their artistic expressions found in catacombs. Understanding this era's social dynamics is crucial since class distinctions often influenced burial practices and thus affected who had access to more elaborate decorations within their tombs. Additionally, examining societal attitudes towards death provides insight into why certain motifs like banquets or pastoral scenes were popular—they reflected hopes for an afterlife filled with abundance or tranquility.

Chapter Twenty

Preserving and Accessing the Legacy of Catacomb Art

Conservation Efforts to Protect Fragile Catacomb Paintings

The catacombs, with their ancient and fragile paintings, are a testament to the early Christian community's faith and resilience. These subterranean burial sites not only served as resting places for the dead but also as sanctuaries for worship and safe havens during periods of persecution. The conservation of these delicate artworks is a complex task that requires a multifaceted approach. One of the primary challenges in preserving catacomb paintings is the environment itself. The constant threat of humidity, temperature fluctuations, and microbial growth can cause deterioration over time. To combat these issues, conservators employ climate control systems designed to maintain stable conditions within the catacombs. These systems often include dehumidifiers, air filters, and temperature regulators that work in concert to create an optimal preservation environment.

In addition to environmental controls, conservationists use advanced techniques to stabilize and restore the paintings themselves. This may involve consolidating flaking paint using specialized adhesives or employing laser cleaning methods to gently remove centuries of grime without damaging the underlying artwork. In some cases, conservators must also address structural issues within the catacombs that could pose risks to the paintings, such as reinforcing weakened walls or ceilings. Another aspect of conservation involves monitoring and research. Teams of experts regularly assess the condition of catacomb art through visual inspections and technological tools like infrared thermography and 3D scanning. These assessments help identify potential problems before they become critical, allowing for timely interventions. Despite these efforts, there are instances where direct intervention is not possible or advisable due to the risk of further damage. In such cases, conservators may opt for preventive measures like installing barriers to protect paintings from human contact or creating detailed documentation so that knowledge of these works persists even if they cannot be saved physically.

Digitization Projects for Increased Accessibility to Catacomb Art

As physical access to catacomb art poses both conservation risks and practical challenges due to their subterranean nature and fragility, digitization projects have emerged as vital tools for increasing accessibility while preserving these historical treasures. Digitization initiatives involve capturing high-resolution images or creating 3D models of catacomb spaces and their artworks. One pioneering project in this field is the Vatican's collaboration with various technology companies to scan parts of the Roman Catacombs using laser scanners and advanced photographic techniques. These digital reproductions allow scholars worldwide unprecedented access to study frescoes in minute detail without ever setting foot inside the actual catacombs.

Beyond academic study, digitization opens up educational opportunities for broader audiences. Virtual tours enable people from all walks of life to explore these ancient sites from their homes or classrooms through immersive experiences provided by virtual reality (VR) platforms or online databases showcasing high-quality images accompanied by scholarly commentary. These digital archives also serve as a safeguard against loss due to natural disasters or other unforeseen events that could damage or destroy physical sites. By maintaining comprehensive digital records, we ensure future generations can experience this heritage regardless of what happens in the physical world. Digitization projects often go hand-in-hand with public outreach programs aimed at raising awareness about the importance of preserving cultural heritage sites like catacombs. Crowdfunding campaigns have been launched alongside digitization efforts not only to fund technology costs but also engage communities directly in preservation activities.

Exhibitions, Museums, and Educational Initiatives Showcasing Catacomb Art

Catacomb art has found its way into museums around the world through exhibitions designed specifically around early Christian artifacts recovered from these underground burial places. Such exhibitions offer visitors a glimpse into early Christianity's spiritual life while highlighting ongoing preservation efforts. Museums play a crucial role in educating public audiences about historical contexts surrounding catacomb art by curating displays that combine original artifacts with replicas created using modern technologies like 3D printing— allowing hands-on interaction without risking damage to originals.

Educational initiatives extend beyond museum walls into classrooms where teachers use reproductions or digital resources as teaching aids about early Christian history and artistry found within catacombs' confines— bringing history alive for students who might never visit Rome themselves. Furthermore, special programs are sometimes organized around major exhibitions where lectures by historians or workshops on ancient painting techniques provide deeper engagement opportunities for those interested in learning more about this unique form of religious expression from antiquity. Conservation efforts focus on maintaining stable environmental conditions within catacombs while employing cutting-edge restoration techniques when necessary. Digitization projects facilitate global access without compromising artifact integrity—serving both scholarly pursuits and general interest. Exhibitions at museums along with educational initiatives bring awareness about this rich cultural legacy while fostering appreciation among diverse audiences worldwide.

Challenges of Preserving Catacomb Art

Preserving and safeguarding the integrity of catacomb art is no easy task. There are numerous challenges that arise, threatening the long-term preservation of these valuable historical treasures. In this subchapter, we will discuss the various challenges faced in preserving catacomb art and delve into the reasons behind their vulnerability. One of the primary challenges in preserving catacomb art lies in the environmental factors that can cause deterioration. The underground conditions of the catacombs, such as high humidity levels and temperature fluctuations, create an inhospitable environment for the art. The constant exposure to moisture and the lack of proper ventilation can lead to the growth of mold, fungi, and algae on the surfaces of the artworks. This not only affects their aesthetic appearance but also weakens the structural integrity of the art, making it more susceptible to damage.

Tourism also poses a significant threat to catacomb art. With thousands of tourists visiting the catacombs each year, the increased foot traffic can cause wear and tear on the delicate art pieces. Visitors unintentionally brushing against the walls, touching the artwork, or even accidental collisions can result in scratches, abrasions, and other forms of damage. Furthermore, the presence of large crowds can also lead to elevated levels of humidity and temperature within the catacombs, accelerating the deterioration process. Another challenge faced in preserving catacomb art is vandalism. Unfortunately, there have been instances where individuals have defaced and damaged the art for various reasons, such as graffiti or theft. These acts of vandalism not only destroy the historical value of the artworks but also disrupt the overall atmosphere and sanctity of the catacombs. The delicate nature of the art makes it difficult to restore and repair once it has been damaged, further emphasizing the importance of safeguarding against such acts.

Preserving catacomb art requires a diligent and proactive approach. Environmental factors, tourism, and vandalism all pose significant threats to the integrity of these historical treasures. By raising awareness, implementing protective measures, and adopting conservation techniques, we can ensure that future generations have the opportunity to experience and appreciate the beauty and significance of catacomb art.

Modern Techniques for Restoration

In the restoration of catacomb art, modern techniques have played a significant role in preserving and showcasing the timeless beauty of these ancient masterpieces. By employing innovative methods, art restorers have been able to bring new life to these once-faded artworks, allowing us to appreciate the intricate details and historical significance they hold. One of the key techniques used in the restoration of catacomb art is digital imaging. Through the use of advanced technology, high-resolution images of the artwork are captured and analyzed. This allows restorers to identify minute details that may have been obscured over time, such as brushstrokes or hidden layers of paint. These digital images serve as valuable references throughout the restoration process, ensuring that every restoration decision is based on the most accurate information available.

Another important technique in catacomb art restoration is laser cleaning. Traditional methods of removing dirt and grime, such as scrubbing or chemical treatments, can be damaging to fragile artworks. Laser cleaning, however, offers a precise and gentle way to remove surface contaminants without causing any harm to the original artwork. By adjusting the wavelength and intensity of the laser, restorers can remove dirt particles layer by layer, revealing the true colors and textures beneath. Additionally, the use of 3D printing has revolutionized the restoration process. When fragments or missing sections of an artwork are discovered, restorers can now create precise replicas using 3D printing technology. These replicas can then be seamlessly integrated into the original artwork, giving viewers a more complete and immersive experience of the original composition.

In the restoration of catacomb art, ethical considerations and conservation principles play a vital role in ensuring the preservation of these historically significant artworks for future generations. Restorers must carefully navigate the delicate balance between preserving the original integrity of the artwork and making necessary interventions to stabilize and protect it from further deterioration. One key ethical consideration is the principle of minimal intervention. Restorers strive to intervene as little as possible, focusing on stabilizing the artwork rather than altering or enhancing its original state. This approach ensures that the historical authenticity of the artwork is preserved, allowing viewers to experience and appreciate the artwork as it was intended by its creator.

Another important ethical consideration is the use of reversible materials and techniques. Restorers aim to use materials and methods that can be easily undone in the future, should new restoration techniques or knowledge become available. This ensures that future generations of restorers have the flexibility to make further improvements without causing irreversible damage to the artwork. Conservation principles, such as environmental monitoring and preventive conservation, are also integral to the restoration process. By closely monitoring temperature, humidity, and lighting conditions, restorers can create an environment that minimizes the risk of deterioration. Additionally, preventive measures, such as proper handling and display techniques, are implemented to prolong the lifespan of these fragile artworks.

Modern Techniques for Restoration

Ancient catacomb art holds immense historical and cultural significance, and its restoration requires the use of modern techniques to ensure its preservation. In recent years, advancements in technology have revolutionized the restoration process, allowing for more accurate analysis and delicate interventions. One such technique is multispectral imaging, which uses different wavelengths of light to capture detailed images of the artwork. By analyzing the reflected or transmitted light, restorers are able to identify hidden layers, pigments, or structural weaknesses that may not be visible to the naked eye. This technique provides invaluable insights into the artwork's composition and condition, aiding in the decision-making process for restoration interventions.

Another modern technique is micro-CT scanning, which allows for non-invasive examination of the artwork's internal structures. By creating detailed 3D models, restorers can analyze the materials used, identify any structural damage, or even discover hidden fragments that may have been lost over time. This information is essential for making informed decisions about the appropriate restoration techniques and materials to be used. Laser ablation is yet another innovative technique used in the restoration of catacomb art. By precisely removing layers of dirt or unwanted overpaint, restorers can reveal the original artwork while minimizing the risk of damage. Laser ablation offers a gentle and controlled approach to cleaning, allowing restorers to remove surface contaminants without affecting the underlying paint layers. These modern techniques, combined with the expertise and skills of art restorers, have revolutionized the restoration of catacomb art. Through their careful and meticulous efforts, these ancient masterpieces can be preserved for future generations to appreciate and learn from.

Controversies in Restoration

When it comes to the restoration of catacomb art, there are ongoing debates and controversies surrounding the topic. In this subchapter, we will delve into some of these controversies and explore the different perspectives on restoration. One of the main controversies surrounding the restoration of catacomb art is the issue of authenticity. Some argue that restoring the art alters its original form and can potentially diminish its historical value. They believe that the natural decay and aging of the artwork is part of its charm and should be preserved. On the other hand, proponents of restoration argue that preserving the art in its deteriorated state can lead to further deterioration and eventual loss of the artwork. They believe that restoration can help protect and prolong the lifespan of these cultural heritage pieces.

Another controversy surrounding restoration is the choice of materials and techniques used. There is an ongoing debate about whether modern materials and techniques are suitable for restoring ancient artwork. Some purists argue that only traditional methods should be employed, as they closely resemble the techniques used during the time the artwork was created. Others believe that modern materials and techniques can achieve better results in terms of durability and visual appearance. Furthermore, there is a debate over the extent of restoration that should be carried out. Some argue for minimal intervention, only addressing major structural damages and stabilizing the artwork. They believe that any additional restoration may alter the original character and intention of the artist. On the contrary, proponents of extensive restoration argue that fully restoring the artwork can bring it back to its former glory and allow viewers to appreciate it as it was intended. These controversies highlight the challenges faced when it comes to the restoration of catacomb art. The decisions surrounding restoration require careful consideration of the historical value, artistic integrity, and preservation of these invaluable cultural heritage pieces.

Uncovering Hidden Treasures

Rediscovery of Forgotten Artistic Gems

Throughout history, there have been numerous instances where art and artifacts of immense historical and cultural value have been forgotten or overlooked. In the realm of Christian art, one such example is the art found in the catacombs beneath the city of Rome. These underground burial sites were used by early Christians to honor their deceased loved ones and practice their faith during times of persecution. In recent years, there has been a resurgence of interest in these catacombs and the artwork they contain. Scholars and art historians have dedicated themselves to exploring and rediscovering these forgotten artistic gems, shedding light on a rich and vibrant period in Christian history. With advancements in technology, such as high-resolution imaging and 3D scanning, researchers have been able to uncover intricate details of the artwork that were previously unseen. This has allowed for a deeper understanding and appreciation of the artistic techniques and symbolism employed by the early Christian artists.

One of the key factors contributing to the rediscovery of these artistic treasures is the meticulous documentation and cataloging of the catacomb sites. Scholars have meticulously examined each fresco, sculpture, and inscription, piecing together the stories and beliefs of the early Christian communities. Furthermore, these rediscovered artworks have provided valuable insights into the lives and beliefs of early Christians. The catacomb art depicts scenes from the Bible, such as the Good Shepherd, the Last Supper, and the Resurrection, providing a glimpse into the faith and spirituality of these early believers. Not only do these findings shed light on the religious practices of the early Christians, but they also serve as a form of Christian apologetics. The art found in the catacombs provides evidence of the existence and perseverance of the early Christian communities in the face of persecution and adversity.

Overall, the rediscovery and reevaluation of the forgotten art in the catacombs is a testament to the power of modern scholarship and technology. Through these efforts, we are able to appreciate and learn from the artistic treasures that were once hidden from view. The exploration of the catacomb art offers a window into the past, allowing us to better understand and connect with the early Christian communities who left behind these remarkable works of art.

Revelations from Ongoing Exploration

Explorations and excavations in the Christian Catacombs have yielded remarkable findings and provided invaluable insights into the history of Christianity. This ongoing research has shed light on the lives and beliefs of early Christians, as well as the artistic and cultural expressions of their faith. One of the most fascinating revelations from these ongoing explorations is the abundance of Christian art found within the catacombs. The walls of the burial chambers are adorned with intricate frescoes and sculptures that depict scenes from the Bible, as well as symbols of faith such as the fish and the Chi-Rho. These artworks not only serve as reminders of the early Christians' devotion, but also provide a visual representation of their beliefs and values.

The ongoing excavations have uncovered a wealth of archaeological evidence that further corroborates the historical accuracy of biblical accounts. Ancient artifacts, such as inscriptions and funerary epitaphs, have been found, offering valuable insights into the lives and customs of the early Christian communities. These discoveries serve as tangible proof of the existence and endurance of early Christian traditions and practices. Furthermore, the explorations in the Christian Catacombs have provided a deeper understanding of the symbolism and significance of these underground burial sites. The catacombs, with their labyrinthine corridors and interconnected chambers, were not only a place of internment but also served as gathering spaces for Christian worship and communal gatherings. The architecture and layout of the catacombs reveal the central role of Christianity in the lives of the early believers.

Overall, the ongoing explorations and excavations in the Christian Catacombs have offered an unparalleled glimpse into the early Christian world. These findings and insights challenge and expand existing knowledge by providing a more comprehensive understanding of the history, art, and culture of early Christianity. The ongoing research in the catacombs continues to unlock the secrets and mysteries of the past, allowing us to appreciate and admire the resilience and devotion of the early Christian communities.

The Fascination with Buried Art

Throughout history, humans have been captivated by the idea of buried treasure. Whether it be gold, jewels, or ancient artifacts, the allure of uncovering hidden treasures has always held a certain fascination. But perhaps one of the most intriguing forms of buried art is that which can be found in ancient catacombs. Christian apologetics refers to the defense of the Christian faith using rational arguments and evidence. One area where Christian apologetics shines is in the study of Christian history and the preservation of ancient Christian artwork. The catacombs, in particular, offer a unique opportunity to examine the art and history of early Christianity. The Christian catacombs were underground burial chambers used by early Christians to bury their dead. These catacombs hold thousands of graves and are adorned with beautiful frescoes, sculptures, and inscriptions that depict scenes from the Bible and the lives of early Christians. They serve as a tangible connection to the past, allowing us to glimpse into the world of early Christianity and understand the art and beliefs of this time.

One reason why buried art has such enduring fascination is the mystery and anticipation it carries. The idea of uncovering hidden treasures and lost secrets appeals to our sense of adventure and curiosity. It is like peering into a time capsule, where each artifact has a story to tell and holds the potential to change our understanding of the past. Another reason for the fascination with buried art is the cultural and historical value it holds. Artifacts found in the catacombs provide valuable insights into the customs, beliefs, and traditions of early Christians. They give us a glimpse into their way of life, their values, and their understanding of faith. By studying these artworks, we can better understand the origins and development of Christianity as a religion. The aesthetic value of buried art is also significant. The frescoes and sculptures found in the catacombs demonstrate the skill and creativity of the artists of ancient times. They depict vivid scenes from the Bible, such as miracles performed by Jesus and stories from the Old Testament. These artworks not only serve as religious symbols but also as expressions of beauty and artistic excellence.

In conclusion, the fascination with buried art, especially in Christian catacombs, stems from the mystery and anticipation it carries, as well as the cultural, historical, and aesthetic value it holds. It allows us to connect with the past, gain insights into the history and beliefs of ancient societies, and appreciate the artistic achievements of our ancestors.

Chapter Twenty-Two

Unanswered Questions and Future Directions for Research

Unsolved Mysteries Surrounding Specific Pieces or Themes in Catacomb Art

The catacombs of ancient Rome are a labyrinthine network of underground burial places that hold not only the remains of early Christians but also a treasure trove of art. This art, rich with symbols and narratives, provides an invaluable glimpse into the beliefs and practices of early Christianity. However, despite extensive study, many aspects remain shrouded in mystery. One such enigma is the interpretation of specific iconographic themes that recur throughout catacomb art. For instance, the image of the Good Shepherd is pervasive, often depicted as a youthful figure carrying a sheep across his shoulders. While it's widely accepted as a representation of Christ's pastoral care for his followers, some scholars suggest it may also contain layers of meaning related to pastoral leadership within the early church community or even be an adaptation from earlier pagan imagery.

Another unresolved question pertains to the depiction of seemingly secular scenes from daily life or mythology alongside overtly Christian symbols. The presence of these images raises questions about their significance and how they were reconciled with Christian teachings by those who commissioned and created them. Furthermore, there are cryptic inscriptions accompanying some pieces whose meanings have been lost to time. These inscriptions could potentially offer insights into theological debates or social dynamics within the early Christian communities but remain undeciphered due to linguistic evolution or lack of context.

The use of certain motifs like the peacock, which is believed to symbolize immortality due to an ancient myth that its flesh does not decay after death, poses another intriguing puzzle. The extent to which such symbolism was understood and embraced by common believers versus being an intellectual exercise among more educated Christians is still debated. In addition to these thematic mysteries, technical questions about methods and materials used in creating catacomb art persist. The origins and trade routes for pigments used in frescoes, for example, could reveal much about cultural exchanges during this period.

New Discoveries and Ongoing Excavations in the Field of Early Christian Archaeology

Early Christian archaeology continues to evolve with new discoveries that reshape our understanding of this formative period in history.

Ongoing excavations yield fresh data on how early Christians lived, worshipped, and buried their dead. Recent finds include previously unknown catacombs or sections thereof which had been sealed off or forgotten over centuries. These discoveries often come with unique artwork or inscriptions that provide new perspectives on early Christian iconography and language usage. Technological advancements have revolutionized archaeological methods; ground-penetrating radar (GPR) allows researchers to survey areas without disturbing them physically. This non-invasive approach has led to the identification of potential sites for excavation while preserving their integrity until they can be explored responsibly. Moreover, bioarchaeological analysis has become increasingly important in studying human remains found within catacombs. Through DNA sequencing and isotopic analysis, scientists can now trace lineage patterns, migration habits, diet composition—even diseases prevalent among early Christian populations—offering a more nuanced picture of their daily lives.

Additionally, interdisciplinary collaborations between archaeologists, historians, theologians, linguists, and other specialists are yielding richer interpretations than any single field could achieve alone. For instance, comparative studies between different regions' burial practices have illuminated variations in ritualistic behaviors reflecting theological diversity within early Christianity.

Exploring Connections between Modern Christianity and the Legacy of Catacombs

The legacy left by ancient catacombs extends far beyond historical curiosity; it resonates deeply with modern Christianity on multiple levels. As repositories for sacred art and symbols that continue to permeate Christian worship today—the cross being perhaps the most ubiquitous—catacombs serve as physical links connecting contemporary believers with their spiritual ancestors. Modern liturgical practices often draw inspiration from rituals inferred from catacomb art; Eucharistic imagery found on tomb walls echoes through current communion services where bread and wine are consecrated as Christ's body and blood—a tradition spanning millennia back to those very burial chambers.

Moreover, catacombs remind modern Christians about their faith's roots in persecution; they stand as monuments to resilience against oppression—a message particularly poignant in times when religious freedom cannot be taken for granted worldwide. Pilgrimages play an essential role here too; visiting these sacred sites offers believers a tangible connection with history's faithful who practiced under threat yet remained steadfast. Such visits can be profoundly moving experiences that reinforce one's own faith journey through reflection upon past sacrifices made for beliefs held dear today.

Contemporary discussions around death and afterlife find echoes within catacomb walls where hope-filled messages conveyed through art speak across ages about resurrection belief central both then and now within Christianity. Lastly but importantly is education: museums exhibit replicas or original pieces removed from catacombs while virtual reality tours make these inaccessible spaces available online—both serving educational purposes by bringing this aspect of ecclesiastical heritage closer to people unable otherwise engage directly with it thus fostering greater appreciation understanding foundational elements shaping present-day faith expressions globally.

Conclusion

In conclusion, "Art Resurrected from the Catacombs" has offered us a glimpse into the depths of human creativity and expression buried beneath the earth for centuries. As we emerge from these catacombs of history, we carry with us a treasure trove of knowledge about our artistic heritage. But our journey does not end here. Instead, it serves as a launching pad for the future of art and culture. Armed with the insights gleaned from these ancient artworks, we are poised to chart new territories in creativity, innovation, and understanding. The artifacts from the catacombs remind us that art is not merely a reflection of the past, but a beacon guiding us towards a brighter tomorrow. They inspire us to embrace our own artistic impulses and to explore the depths of our imagination without fear or hesitation.

As custodians of this invaluable legacy, it is our responsibility to ensure that these treasures are not consigned to the shadows once more. Rather, we must share them with the world, allowing them to inspire and enrich the lives of future generations. Let us not simply admire the art resurrected from the catacombs, but let us use it as a catalyst for change, a source of inspiration, and a testament to the enduring power of human creativity. Together, let us continue to unearth the wonders of the past as we forge a path towards a brighter, more vibrant future.

Chapter Twenty-Three

About the Author

Wayne Pascall is an accomplished artist with a lifelong passion for creating. His artwork draws inspiration from nature, people, the world around him, and Scriptures from the Bible. Pascall's diverse portfolio includes powerful pieces such as "The Provider," "Love in Paris," and "The Hem of His Garment," which showcase his versatility and depth as an artist. His work often explores spiritual themes, as seen in "The Missing Piece," which symbolically portrays humanity's spiritual void. Pascall offers his art in various formats, including giclée canvas prints, stretched split canvases, acrylic prints, and metal prints, and digital downloads, allowing art enthusiasts to experience his creations in different mediums. With a keen eye for detail and a talent for capturing emotion, Wayne Pascall continues to create thought-provoking and visually stunning artwork that resonates with viewers around the world.

With his artwork featured on various websites, Wayne has touched the lives of countless individuals through his visual storytelling and artistic expression.

To discover Wayne's inspiring artwork, visit:

www.waynepascallart.com

There, you can delve into the vivid world of color, emotion, and imagination that defines his artistic vision.

www.ingramcontent.com/pod-product-compliance
Lightning Source LLC
Chambersburg PA
CBHW031425150726
47989CB00002B/810